Teaching Writing

Teaching Writing

Craft, Art, Genre

Fran Claggett
Sonoma State University

with

Joan Brown
Solano Community College

Nancy Patterson
Grand Valley State University

Louann Reid
Colorado State University

National Council of Teachers of English
1111 W. Kenyon Road, Urbana, Illinois 61801-1096

Materials from Chapters 3 and 4 reprinted by permission from *A Measure of Success* by Fran Claggett. Copyright © 1996 by Mary Frances Claggett. Published by Boynton/Cook, a division of Reed Elsevier, Inc., Portsmouth, NH. All rights reserved.

Student writing from Chapters 3 and 6 reprinted by permission from *Drawing Your Own Conclusions* by Fran Claggett with Joan Brown. Copyright © 1992 by Fran Claggett. Published by Boynton/Cook, a division of Reed Elsevier, Inc., Portsmouth, NH. All rights reserved.

Staff Editor: Bonny Graham

Manuscript Editor: L. L. Erwin

Interior Design: Doug Burnett

Cover Design: Diana C. Coe/kō Design Studio

NCTE Stock Number: 52503

It is the policy of NCTE in its journals and other publications to provide a forum for the open discussion of ideas concerning the content and the teaching of English and the language arts. Publicity accorded to any particular point of view does not imply endorsement by the Executive Committee, the Board of Directors, or the membership at large, except in announcements of policy, where such endorsement is clearly specified.

Every effort has been made to provide current URLs and e-mail addresses, but because of the rapidly changing nature of the Web, some sites and addresses may no longer be accessible.

Library of Congress Cataloging-in-Publication Data

Teaching writing : craft, art, genre / Fran Claggett . . . [et al.].
    p. cm.
    Includes bibliographical references and index.
    ISBN 0-8141-5250-3 (pbk.)
    1. English language—Composition and exercises—Study and teaching (Secondary). 2. English language—Composition and exercises—Study and teaching (Middle school). I. Claggett, Mary Frances.
    LB1631.T34 2005
    808' . 042'0712—dc22
                                                                    2005006962

Dedicated to
Louise M. Rosenblatt
1904–2005

who became, for our profession, the reader, the text, the poem

Etty Hillesum on writing:

Friday evening, 7:30. Looked at Japanese prints with Glassner this afternoon. That's how I want to write. With that much space round a few words. They should simply emphasize the silence. Just like that print with the sprig of blossom in the lower corner. A few delicate brush strokes—but with what attention to the smallest detail—and all around it space, not empty but inspired. The few great things that matter in life can be said in a few words. If I should ever write—but what?—I would like to brush in a few words against a wordless background. To describe the silence and the stillness and to inspire them. What matters is the right relationship between words and wordlessness, the wordlessness in which much more happens than in all the words one can string together. And the wordless background of each short story—or whatever it may be—must have a distinct hue and a discrete content, just like those Japanese prints. It is not some vague and incomprehensible silence, for silence too must have contours and form. All that words should do is to lend the silence form and contours. Each word is like a small milestone, a slight rise in the ground beside a flat, endless road across sweeping plains. It really is quite laughable: I can write whole chapters on how I would like to write, and it is quite possible that apart from these words of wisdom I shall never put pen to paper. But those Japanese prints suddenly showed me most graphically how I would really like to write.

from *An Interrupted Life: The Diaries, 1942–1943; and, Letters from Westerbork,* in which Hillesum chronicles living in Amsterdam during the gradual Nazi encroachment; being sent first to Westerbork, the holding camp; and then boarding the train to Auschwitz.

Contents

Acknowledgments

I first became immersed in the study of genre during my work with Charles Cooper as we designed and implemented the California Assessment Program in the 1980s. With over forty classroom teachers, we analyzed thousands of student papers, seeking the commonalities that defined exemplary work in the genres most frequently taught in middle and high schools. The assessment program included the preparation of handbooks for teaching each of the kinds of writing that we assessed—eight types at grades 8 and 10, with some overlaps. Joan Brown, one of the contributing authors to the genre section of this book, was a major player in the development of the assessment and the handbooks.

Supported by the California Writing Project and the California Literature Project, these handbooks became the groundwork of a statewide movement of teachers teaching teachers. As the handbooks became worn and lost, however, and as new teachers came into the profession, the knowledge gained by the initial collaborative work of both middle and high school teachers became attenuated or buried. It was in response to many requests to update that material that this book was initially conceived. Since then, it has, of course, taken many turns: contributing authors Louann Reid and Nancy Patterson have added significant chapters on strategies for teaching grammar and for integrating computers into the writing classroom.

All of the authors of this book wish to acknowledge some of our great teachers: the innovative thinking and research of James Britton, James Moffett, Louise Rosenblatt, Janet Emig, Donald Graves, John Henry Martin, and others have made visible the practices that give writers power, that focus on acts of writing rather than instruction *about* writing. Judith Langer, Arthur Applebee, Nancie Atwell, Ruth Vinz, Robert Scholes, Leif Fearn, Nancy Farnan, Dan Kirby, and Tom Romano are among those whose practices have informed ours. Most recently, we have been inspired and challenged by the cyberlessons of Ted Nellen, Pat Schulze, and Dawn Hogue, among others, who have extended our vision to think in new ways about teaching writing in the twenty-first century.

No book about teaching is complete without acknowledging how much we have learned from our students. We thank them especially for their willingness to be guinea pigs for our many attempts to try different ways of teaching both reading and writing. Over the years, our students have borne witness to the gigantic changes that have brought us to our present understandings, even knowing as we do that greater understanding awaits us as we continue to learn new ways of trying, in Lu Chi's words, to "know what is and what is not merely fashion. Wanting every word to sing, every writer worries: nothing is ever perfected; no poet can afford to become complacent."

As primary author, I wish to acknowledge and thank the NCTE reviewers, who read the preliminary manuscript very thoroughly and thoughtfully, making many suggestions which I hope they find have improved this revision. I would also like to thank Kurt Austin, Bonny Graham, Lee Erwin, and the rest of the NCTE books program staff for their work to make this book a reality.

I am indebted to Linda Toren, who introduced me to Lu Chi "because the words matter." Written in the third century and elegantly translated by Sam Hamill, Lu Chi's small volume *Wen Fu: The Art of Writing* has provided me with endless knowledge and inspiration.

My final acknowledgment is to Madge Holland, colleague and team-teaching partner, who is the first reader of all my manuscripts.

—Fran Claggett

I Setting Purpose, Finding Form

*Each writer finds a new entrance
into the mystery,
and it is difficult to explain.*

*Nonetheless, I have set down my thinking
as clearly as I can.*

The Art of Writing: Lu Chi's Wen Fu

About This Book . . .

This book is designed to contain, in Wallace Stevens's words, "pages of possibilities." It is intended to be a writing teacher's resource, a book to help you sort through and make sense of some things we have learned about the teaching of writing: about making choices; about rethinking the use of genres; about reenvisioning the role of craft; about teaching not only the craft but also the art of writing. Ultimately, it is about setting purpose and finding form.

Our goal is students who are confident and effective writers, especially but not only in these times of high-stakes testing and legislative mandates that threaten to narrow the curriculum. Enormous industries have been built up around the testing industry, encompassing not only the tests but also the expensive scoring of tests, the promotion of textbooks and Web sites designed to accompany the books, and consultants hired by districts to provide inservice to teachers on preparing students for the bombardment of multiple tests and measurements. Districts that use the professional expertise of the teacher to empower students honor that expertise by providing time and resources for teachers to help students learn the craft of writing through sound instruction. We believe that teachers who teach from a sound philosophical base will not only be more effective classroom teachers but will also be able to work more productively in the larger political/professional sphere to accommodate thoughtfully constructed standards and resist the testing of minutiae. Tests that demand compliance regardless of educational validity suck hours out of every school year, reducing the actual learning time of students and giving priority to false values.

We look at how writing is used in the workplace today and know that what we teach must help students survive not only in the current test-driven political climate but also in the marketplace, where students will need to write effective office memos or notes from meetings or projects that need careful attention to detail. They will be writing personal e-mail notes that have become a way of staying in touch for great numbers of people. They will be posting notes to friends and colleagues on the Internet. While many districts are buying and mandating scripted programs that claim validation from scientific research, others are looking for approaches that honor the essential purpose of writing—communication, in all its diverse forms.

We see too many people, even within the field, who are either resigned to or comfortable with teaching to the test. In such classrooms, students are more likely to be taught *about* writing—rules of grammar and usage, spelling and punctuation—than they are to have opportunities to write for their own purposes, to write for audiences beyond the classroom, to write because they have something to say to someone specific.

Yet we have also seen classrooms where teachers are *not* telling the students what to do. These are classrooms where the question is not "How do I prepare my students for these tests?" but "How do I help students know what writing options are available to them and know how to make decisions about which options to use at a particular time?" This question implies a rethinking of how to incorporate the understanding of genres into our writing program. Some of our best teaching, measured by student learning, occurs when we support students in their endeavors to find the best way to express *their* ideas, to take ownership for what they write. While we affirm that the act of writing promotes students' discovery and knowledge about their own writing, it is our premise that there is a fine but critical line between having students "just write" and giving them the guidance that will help them make appropriate choices in their own writing.

Writing as a Craft

Central to the ideas and approaches in this book is the idea that writing is a craft that can be taught, can be learned, can be improved with guided instruction. Inherent in this idea is the recognition that writing involves decision making. At every turn writers make choices—about purpose, subject, audience, language, form, and details. Decision making, with its built-in correlative of questioning, emerges as a fundamental strategy to help students move from novice to experienced writers. Since we know from metacognitive research that being aware of choices and their effects helps make writers independent, we should place decision making at the forefront of our teaching, even as we incorporate all the other aspects of writing instruction.

Writing as an Art

Since we are teachers of English, it is almost axiomatic that we love literature. We understand not only the craft of writing but also the art. We look with dismay at student textbooks that present writing as a hierarchy of skills that must be mastered in order to produce a perfect formulaic series of paragraphs. We seek out those books and programs that are true to our knowledge: that writing is an art we can help our students aspire to. In the best writing classrooms, writing is treated as both a craft and an art. Louise Rosenblatt's explanation of efferent and aesthetic reading and writing demonstrates how purpose is central to both the craft and the art of writing.

Teaching Writing, Too, Is Both a Craft and an Art

Just as writing is both a craft and an art—complex, often nonlinear in its process—so is the teaching of writing. We must be teachers who are constantly examining what good writing is and who can help students get involved in the exploration. At the same time, we must not depend on artificial structures that ultimately reduce the act of composition to formulaic practices. We must be teachers who value reading as a way of internalizing options in writing, who help students read as writers. We must be teachers who hone our own craft as teachers—and as readers and writers—as we guide students in the art and craft of writing.

And You, the Reader of This Book

Because audience is so important to writers, we have spent some time envisioning you, the audience for this book. We envision you as concerned writing teachers. We believe some of you are teachers new to the profession, drawing on your teacher training as you encounter the realities of classrooms today, filled with students who come with widely disparate needs and preparation. We think some of you are experienced teachers of literature who want to know more about using literature to teach composition. And some of you are experienced teachers of composition who want to know more about how to incorporate literature into your writing programs. All of you are looking for a book that has been framed not only by sound theory and research but also by many productive years in the classroom. We hope that this book is for you.

1 Teaching Writing: An Integrated Approach

Ordering thoughts and ideas,
*   we begin to choose our words.*

The Art of Writing: Lu Chi's Wen Fu

When we titled this opening chapter "Teaching Writing," we were well aware of the distinctions between teaching and learning. Many leaders in the profession are now focusing on the "learning" rather than the "teaching," and we certainly subscribe to the truism that no matter what we attempt to "teach," the only "learning" that transpires belongs to the learner, whether that is student or teacher. Still, we are *teachers*, and the way we interpret that word has everything to do with how and how much learning takes place in our classrooms. That said, we will continue to write about the teaching of writing and hope that our readers will remember that we are always engaged in helping students learn.

Much has been written about different modes of learning since Gabriele Lusser Rico and Fran Claggett first published *Balancing the Hemispheres: Brain Research and the Teaching of Writing*. Howard Gardner's work, beginning with *Frames of Mind*, has provided many researchers and teachers with specific ideas of how to translate his theory of multiple intelligences into practices in education. There is still much to be learned, but we know enough now to design balanced writing programs, ensuring our students opportunities to approach writing from different mental sets.

It is easy to assume that our students process a task the same way we do, but we may be making a false assumption. In order to provide a balanced approach to the teaching of writing, we try to allow for at least two primary modes of processing: on one hand, we provide experiences in clustering, use of color, image making, metaphoric thinking, design. On the other hand, we provide exercises involving sequential thought, precision, step-by-step progression of ideas. We provide opportunities for all students to experience the full range of writing activities, asking them to note which come more naturally, which need to be developed;

which are most appropriate during the initial planning stages, which in the final, editing phases.

One way to think about an integrated approach to the teaching of writing is to adapt James Britton's terminology to discuss modes of writing. Britton uses the terms "expressive, transactional, and poetic" to describe writing that serves different purposes. Expressive writing is informal or casual, usually written for the self, and is typical of letters, journal writing, or freewriting. Transactional writing is writing used to inform, to instruct, or to persuade. Poetic writing, as Britton uses the term, moves into the realm of art, including story, drama, and poem. In an integrated curriculum, we begin with this schema before moving to a range of genres, from persuasion to interpretation to reflection to poetry. By specifically teaching the salient features of many different genres, we teach students not only how to write effective persuasive letters, for instance, but how to adapt and blend genres to suit their specific purposes. We encourage students to find which kind of activity helps them get started, which they need when they step back to revision their work, which to use to bring it into form suitable for publishing.

Writing as Decision Making

For most accomplished writers, the decisions basic to the act of writing have become so completely internalized that they are scarcely aware they are making them. Purpose, audience, point of view, genre or form, length—all are part of the brain's internal decision-making activity before these writers even sit down at the computer. As teachers, we need to help students become aware of what decisions they must make, and how they can learn to make them. As mentioned earlier, research on metacognition shows that being aware of choices and their effects helps in making writers independent. Learning to make choices should be at the forefront of our teaching as we make use of all of the other aspects of writing instruction.

The following chart presents the role of purpose as it affects decisions regarding genre or form. All the other questions—audience, form, point of view, length, and so on, emerge from this central question to form a web of interrelated decisions that guide students in their writing.

The Role of Purpose as It Leads to Various Genres in Writing

Purpose: Personal Exploration (Focus on Writer): to identify, reveal, or clarify ideas or experiences for self or others	Leads to: journal entry, diary, letter, autobiography, poem (Genre focus on, e.g., narrative, memoir)

Purpose: Persuasion (Focus on Reader): to influence or convince another of one's ideas or judgment	Leads to: evaluation, interpretation, critique, editorial, review (Genre focus on, e.g., response to literature, persuasion)

Purpose: Information (Focus on Subject): to convey information; to explain ideas, facts, or processes	Leads to: observation, report, I-Search, field notes, exposition, summary (Genre focus on, e.g., report)

Purpose: Aesthetic Experience (Focus on Craft, Art): to give shape to an experience, observation, or idea	Leads to: story, poem, reflective essay, or any kind of writing elevated to high degree of craft, art (Genre focus on, e.g., reflection, narrative, drama, poetry

Learning from the Masters: The Interrelationship between Reading and Writing

One of the six great principles of Asian brush painting is "emulating the masters." Students spend hours copying the great ink drawings. Only when they have internalized the feel of the brush on paper and succeeded in a painting that appears spontaneous and free do they begin to work on their own. Writers, too, have long acknowledged the powerful effect that emulation, conscious or not, has on their own writing. We know that reading is closely tied to writing. As writing teachers, we can build on this correlation in two ways: encouraging our students to read widely and well, and explicitly teaching them to emulate ways practicing writers achieve their effects. Although the interrelationship between reading and writing is often unstated and subtle, it may, in the classroom, take many forms, such as analyzing what writers do, modeling grammatical structures, transforming texts through exercises in recasting, and conducting extensive style studies, all practices we describe in this book. Part III of this book provides a rationale and practices for modeling. By providing opportunities for writing and instruction in what master writers do, teachers can enhance the time that apprentice writers spend in the act of composing.

Distinguishing between the Terms *Form*, *Formula*, and *Format*

Throughout this book, we present guidelines for writing that depend on an understanding of the terms *form*, *formula*, and *format*. The table below offers a brief overview of these key terms.

Form	intrinsic order	movement of ideas in response to writer's impetus	what emerges from writer's attention to purpose, subject, audience, craft
Formula	externally imposed order	writing in response to given organization	what results from writer's following a prescriptive organization (includes modeling and given poetic forms)
Format	visual or graphic order	attention to setup: spacing, fonts, graphics	what emerges from writer's attention to visual presentation of ideas and information: how the words appear on the page or screen (includes mapping and other kinds of graphic constructions)

The concept of *form* is one that underlies every major discipline; it is the essential structure that enables us to discern the essence of any given element—tree, flower, poem, animal, rock, symphony. Some artists believe that form is innate, in marble, for example, and that the artist releases that essential form by the act of sculpting. In writing, the artist alters and cuts and adds in the ongoing process of revisioning in an effort to come to an artistic rendition of the poem, essay, story that expresses its essential form. In school, we rarely have the opportunity to work on the grand scale of artistic vision, but the writers of this book believe that every person can approach the idea of form with understanding. As teachers, we provide opportunities to discover form, whether by working from the outside in or the inside out.

While generally we caution against formulaic patterns for generating writing assignments, we do support specific strategies that involve the use of *formula*. We have seen too many charts in classrooms around the country that depict "The Writing Process" with bold arrows showing a linear movement from *drafting* to *revising* to *editing*, a formula that denies the recursive aspect of writing. We understand the urge to teach genre structures in a formulaic way, but teaching persuasion, for instance, from the starting point of purpose, and coming to form through making decisions based on an understanding of a potential audience, is quite different from teaching students to fill in the outline of "the" persuasive essay. Examples of how to teach persuasion in an organic way are given in Chapter 4.

On the other hand, we propose that modeling, recasting, and transforming teach the concept of form through assignments that are to some degree formulaic. In working with writing at the sentence and paragraph levels, as elucidated in Chapter 10, "Teaching Grammar in Contexts *for* Writing," you will see some exercises that use formulaic exercises to generate original work that leads to understanding of grammatical forms. In Chapter 8, too, we note that when students write poems such as haiku, sonnets, villanelles, and sestinas, they work within the formulaic strictures of given forms. As contemporary poets demonstrate, however, even the traditional form of the sonnet is open to many degrees of variation.

The concept of *format* as we use it in this book is a way of presenting ideas graphically. Format may refer to mapping or metaphoric graphics (see, for example, the lesson on writing memoir, Chapter 7). It may also mean simply paying attention to fonts and font sizes or just the white space on the page. We all know that the format of a book makes a lot of difference in how inviting it is to pick up and read. By teaching students the importance of format in presenting their ideas, we are helping them develop their spatial intelligence, a quality in ever greater demand in the workplace. One of our students recently reported that she has carved a very lucrative position for herself by mapping and graphing business meetings and seminars as they are going on. Her experience with mapping in high school led her directly to seeing how this ability could provide a service in the business world. Nancy Patterson's chapter, "Join the E-Generation: Integrating Computers into the Writing Classroom," demonstrates clearly how the process of formatting for the Web helps students understand and present their ideas.

Understanding Style and Voice

The idea of *voice* in writing is subject to a lot of discussion among teachers. If you examine a bookshelf filled with books on writing or the teaching of writing, however, you may see a book that deals exclusively with voice and others that do not mention voice in the entire book. Certainly teachers know what they mean by the concept of *voice*. We remember saying to our students, "We should be able to identify your papers by the voice in the writing whether your names appear on them or not." The concept of *voice* appears in most rubrics, from the Six Traits rubric to the New Standards rubrics[1] to many state rubrics. Some researchers, however, refuse to use the word because it is vague, difficult to define. But if we, as teachers, understand what we mean by *voice*, then we must be able to talk about how to teach it.

We propose that *voice* is inextricably linked to *style*. We posit that it emerges from a writer's particular way of constructing sentences, of using clusters of words that point to a way of perceiving the world. Style has been described in some rubrics as comprising diction and sentence structure. Rise Axelrod and Charles Cooper, in the *St. Martin's Guide to Writing*, have no index reference to *voice*, but devote fifteen pages to "Editing for Style." Loosely, they refer to style as "the way you say something," and then go on to say that "good style [. . .] is an art. As such, it cannot be taught through the study of rules. Writers develop a style by caring about the way they express themselves, by paying attention to the style of other writers, and by being willing to experiment with different possibilities for putting a thought into words" (633). They then discuss many of the elements of style that can, in fact, be identified in a piece of writing, offering substantive suggestions for ways to recast stylistically inept sentences.

"Our habits make our style," Josephine Miles once wrote about the composing process. Believing that to be true, in writing as well as in life, we feel responsible for helping our students cultivate writing habits that will help them develop their own styles, be evident in the voices we hear when we read their work. An integrated approach to teaching writing involves more than lip service to the expression that reading and writing are flip sides of the same coin. It goes much deeper. In a truly integrated approach, we view writing as an act of composing and interpreting, and reading as an act of interpreting and composing. As teachers of writing, we must be both composers and interpreters of our own work.

Note

1. New Standards is a joint project of the National Center of Education and the Economy and the University of Pittsburgh, underway since 1991.

2 Vision and Revision

Only through writing and then revising
and revising
may one gain the necessary insight.

The Art of Writing: Lu Chi's Wen Fu

This chapter will detail some of the strategies that students may use either as they are getting started or as they hit a point in their writing when they need to look back and think again about what they are doing. We separate this act of *visioning* from the activities we call *revisioning*, which are strategies to use with text already written to provide a different lens for the piece that is taking shape. The term *prewriting*, which became very popular during the early days of the National Writing Project, came to include all of the thinking, doodling, talking about, drawing, clustering, listing, and mapping activities that some writers may do before they begin to organize a piece of writing. We prefer the term *visioning* since these activities may occur either *before* or at any point *during* the writing activity. The early model of a linear process, a set series of stages, soon gave way to an understanding of the recursiveness of the act of writing. Unfortunately, this knowledge did not preclude the continuing prevalence of the linear model in many classrooms.

Visioning Activities

1. Freewriting

Freewriting is, we suspect, more widely used by teachers than it is by writers. In its elemental form, widely popular some years ago, it involved having students write without any specified subject or guidelines for a set amount of time, usually ten minutes. It was first intended as a kind of warm-up activity, a way of increasing fluency for students who had difficulty putting words on paper. It became, however, a kind of ritual in many classrooms, a beginning activity that gave the teacher time to take roll and organize the classroom period.

That concept of freewriting has given way in many classrooms to other kinds of visioning activities: focused freewriting, clustering, mapping, talking, and drawing are all methods of helping students get started on a writing project. With careful assignments, these activities can be useful, but teachers need to think carefully about the purpose of each activity. Furthermore, teachers should explain to students why they are being asked to engage in any of these visioning activities.

Note: For a fuller examination of the place that freewriting has had in teaching writing over the last twenty-five years, see the interview with the author in the Appendix.

2. Clustering

Clustering, as Gabriele Lusser Rico explains in *Writing the Natural Way*, "is a nonlinear brainstorming process akin to free association" (14). Rico describes the origin of her insights into clustering by quoting Northrop Frye, who, observing that words need never be frozen, wrote that "any word [. . .] can become 'a storm center of meanings, sounds, and associations, radiating out indefinitely like ripples in a pool'" (15). She goes on to say, "In a moment of insight, the word 'clustering' popped into my head to describe this radiating phenomenon of nonlinear connections around a 'storm center of meanings' which I call the 'nucleus'" (16).

Clustering involves centering the key word or phrase (Rico's "nucleus"), circling it, then allowing each idea to run its course in a line of related words or ideas. When a new idea occurs, the student begins again at the center and follows the course of associations for this idea. He or she continues this pattern until ideas begin to run out or until one of the ideas becomes very strong. At this point, the student stops clustering and begins writing.

While this technique may be used in many different ways, the most common is to have students cluster a nucleus word or phrase for ten minutes several times a week. By moving directly from the cluster to writing, students soon find themselves writing brief, tightly constructed paragraphs marked by strong use of specific details. The benefit of the clustering comes from the spatial arrangement of the cluster in contrast to the linear arrangement of the typical brainstormed list.

Once students have become fluent in moving from cluster to writing, the teacher can refine the activity. One method is to have students color-code the different grammatical constructions they used in their clusters, or to have them color-code abstract and concrete words (more on that topic in the section on recasting). In the former, students observe whether they were focusing on description (if they used primarily nouns and adjectives) or events (if they used a preponderance of verbs). Students then can pursue writing in the appropriate genre to take advantage of their cluster words. It is useful to have students work in pairs to discuss how their minds were operating during the clustering process and how they moved into writing from the cluster.

Rico writes, "Too many of us get stuck because we *think* we should know where to start and which ideas to develop. When we find we don't, we become anxious and either force things or quit. We forget to wonder, leaving ourselves open to what might come. Wondering means it's acceptable not to know. It is the natural state at the beginning of all creative acts, as recent brain research shows." (15)

Revisioning Activities

To talk about revision, we need to take the word apart: *re-vision*. We will deal with revision here as *recasting,* based on a revisioning of the written text. There are many ways to recast a text with an eye toward making a piece stronger, more powerful, more accurate. Before a writer can revision a text effectively, however, the writer needs to think about *purpose,* which is inextricably tied up with *audience.* Unless the writer addresses these aspects of the writing, revision is a fruitless, mechanical, rarely successful attempt to bring the words in line with some abstract concept of correctness. The following exercises, approached in a positive way, can help writers learn to look at their writing with new eyes.

Beginning the Revisioning Process

- Short pieces: We suggest beginning the process with short pieces, no more than one side of one page, whether prose or poetry. One of the things we have learned from brain research is that many students lose the sense of the whole when working with a longer piece. We have found that to be especially true with students who have learning problems; they turn the page and it's all new. When they can see the whole on one side of one page, they make great progress in seeing overall structure as well as how parts work together.

- Voice: Choose assignments that are designed to involve the writer using his or her own voice—autobiographical incidents, sketches, reflective or speculative pieces.

- Language as play: Approach the recastings in a lighthearted spirit, almost as a game. Have students work with a partner so that they can bounce ideas around. If possible, provide each pair with a thesaurus.

- Preparation: For the *language recastings*, you may need to do some preparatory teaching about the forms of the verb "to be," about modifiers, or about concrete and abstract nouns.

An Exercise in Recasting Content: Intent and Perception

Directions for students working with partners to recast:

> Exchange your writing with a partner. The partner reads your writing, then tells you what it says. (Alternatively, the partner writes what it says in his or her own words.) Compare what your partner says with what you think your piece says. If there are any differences, look at the words together and see how you can make your intent and the reader's perceptions match. If you like what your partner heard better than what you thought you were saying, work together to change your plan. See how you can strengthen that meaning. You don't need to stay with your first ideas.

An Exercise in Recasting Form: Prose Recast as Poetry

You can model this process for your students using the board or an overhead. Begin with a very short prose piece. Then, picking out words and phrases that create strong images, write them on the board in lines. Keep the intent of the prose piece, but delete all words which do not contribute directly to the meaning. Read the finished poem and compare it to the original prose piece. Give it a title.

> Directions for students:

> Begin with a piece of prose, no longer than one page. Rewrite it as a poem. How? Pick out words and phrases you like, especially phrases that create a strong picture in your mind. Write them on separate lines. Add any words you want. Compare your prose and poem versions. Decide which form you like best for what you want to say. You may want to rewrite your prose version, taking out superfluous words to make it sound more forceful.

Other possibilities for recasting form might involve rewriting the piece as a dialogue or full script, with stage directions.

An Exercise in Recasting Point of View: Story, Biography, or Autobiography

Directions for students:

> Begin with a story, firsthand biography, or autobiographical incident. Think about the point of view you took when you wrote this piece. Who else is in the story? How did it appear to this person? Rewrite the story from that other person's point of view.

Exercises in Recasting Language

Exercise A: Recasting by Replacing All Forms of the Verb "To Be"

On the board, make a list for your students of the present and past forms of the forms of the verb *to be: am, are, is, was, were.*

Directions for students:

> Rewrite your piece without using any of these words. You may need to change whole sentences to do this. When you finish, look at both versions with a partner. See which parts you like better as they were and which you like better the new way. Write a final version using whatever words you want.

Exercise B: Recasting by Reducing the Number of Modifiers

Directions for recasting without modifiers:

> Circle all of the modifiers you used on your first draft. Rewrite your piece without any of these modifiers. Try to get the same effect by using strong verbs. Use the thesaurus. With a partner, compare the two versions. See where, in the second version, you really need to use a modifier. Put it back in if you need it. Make a final version using only those modifiers that are important.

Exercise C: Recasting Nouns by Replacing Abstractions with Concrete Images

This one-period activity provides an introduction for your students to the concepts *abstract* and *concrete.* You can introduce it at some point when you are having students write about specific values, emotions, or themes, as they do in Chapter 7, on memoir. Work through the following graphic assignment for making an abstraction concrete before using this recasting strategy.

The process for "making an abstraction concrete" involves generating a list of abstractions, preferably related either to a writing assignment or to a study of a novel or poem. Or you might generate the list from students' responses to the writing assignment, in order to focus on some of the important values or feelings in their lives.

Supposing they suggest *power, frustration, selflessness.* We then ask them to think about how to *draw* their abstract words. What concrete images could exemplify their abstractions? What is *power* like, for example? They begin to doodle images. One student draws a sword. Another a broken umbrella. Why a sword? "Power is like a two-edged sword," the student responds. We move then from the simile to the straightforward, more forceful metaphor: "Power *is* a two-edged sword," one student quickly replies. "Frustration *is* a broken umbrella in a hard rain," someone adds, moving from her drawing directly to the metaphor.

With plain white paper and lots of colored markers available, students next choose one abstraction from their own lists and begin drawing.

When they have finished their drawings (ten minutes is enough for this activity), they first title the drawing with the name of the abstraction. Then they write an extended metaphor, which often takes the shape of a short poem. In this sequence the subtleties of the metaphor emerge: abstraction, drawing, a sentence containing an elaboration of the initial concrete image.

Now students are ready to return to their own papers. Directions to the student for the exercise:

> Now, working with a paper you want to revise, identify all of the nouns in your piece. How specific are they? Try to find a specific or concrete noun for each general or abstract noun you have used. Rewrite, using specific nouns whenever possible. When you keep an abstract noun, you must know it is important.

An Overview of the Revisioning Process

Students often think a first draft is a finished piece. Occasionally it is. More often, however, it is the beginning phase of a process that most writers find is the essence of writing. We don't kid ourselves that our students will suddenly want to revise every piece they write; nor should they. But the pieces they do revise should be pieces they have a real investment in. They should have an investment in saying what they have to say in the best possible way. The payoff comes when they discover that what they thought they were going to write isn't what they end up writing at all. Peter Stillman—teacher, editor, poet, short story writer— says in *Families Writing*, "The point is that writing fosters vision (although it's usually, erroneously, put the other way around). It is the most powerful means of discovery accessible to all of us throughout life, which makes it doubly ironic that it is taught and used in schools almost exclusively as a means for printing out what we're already charged with knowing. British novelist E. M. Forster's rhetorical question, quoting an anonymous elderly woman, about writing to discover is familiar to nearly everyone in the writing business: 'How can I know what I think till I see what I say?'" (10).

From Revisioning to Deep Editing

The process generally called *editing* is more complex than it sounds. We hear the admonition that editing should be reserved for the final step before "publication," whatever that entails. In general, we agree: the final step should be a careful *surface editing*, proofreading for typos, errors in spelling, etc. But the larger aspects, *deep editing*—those involving word choice, for instance, or appropriate sentence structure, are, for most writers, folded into the revisioning process.

The following considerations provide a guide to the different aspects of revision that encompass the process of deep editing. In addition to the elements of *surface editing*—spelling, punctuation, capitalization, agreement, etc.—these items deal with the underlying soundness of the piece. In teaching, we suggest focusing on only one item at a time and practicing it on a very short piece, as indicated earlier in this chapter. Later, you can retain that one and add another. Eventually, you can create a checklist from these considerations, modified to suit the age group and sophistication of the students, for them to use during their revisioning process.

Some Considerations for Revisioning

Students learn to select the structures and features of language appropriate to the purpose, audience, and context of the work, demonstrating these qualities:

- an understanding of the interrelationship between sentence construction and appropriate subordination of ideas
  (Note: the difference between a compound sentence and a complex sentence lies in the equation or subordination of ideas);
- appropriate use of diction in writing or speaking in different situations and with different degrees of formality; and
- use of specialized features of language (e.g., metaphor, imagery) in ways that support ideas.

Students learn to analyze and subsequently revise work to clarify it or make it more effective in communicating the intended message or thought through the following deep editing processes:

- adding or deleting details;
- adding or deleting explanations;
- clarifying difficult or obscure passages;
- rearranging words, sentences, and paragraphs to improve or clarify meaning;

- sharpening the focus (usually by deleting superfluous words);
- reconsidering the organizational structure to support the purpose of the piece; and
- rethinking and/or rewriting the piece in light of different audiences and purposes.

Appendix: Freewriting Interview

The following interview with Fran Claggett was initiated by Sarah Nelson, a graduate student of Professor Tom Gage at Humboldt State University. When she set up the interview, she was working on a research project to assess what kinds of pedagogical value freewriting has in contemporary classrooms.

> *Sarah:* First, I was hoping that you could just tell me a little about yourself and your relationship with freewriting either personally or professionally.

> *Fran:* I was a high school teacher for many years. I have also taught from time to time at the university level, but briefly each time. I have been consulting, first through the Writing Project, then on my own, since the mid-eighties. I have written several books for teachers and was coauthor of the *Daybooks of Critical Reading and Writing*. My true love is poetry and I have one (old, now) book of poems. Maybe when I stop working, I'll have another one. I'm not consulting as much as I used to, but I am working on a book on teaching writing for NCTE, if I ever get to it! I've been writing lots of curriculum units for the National Center on Education and the Economy and also for the Denver schools. What else? Oh yes, assessment. I was the facilitator for the development of the California Assessment Program and the California Learning Assessment System tests. On those assessments, by the way, we built in time for focused freewriting to help students generate writing their essays.

> *Sarah:* When did you start using freewriting in your teaching?

> *Fran:* Trying to think back to when freewriting became part of teaching writing . . . Certainly it was before the Writing Project began in 1974. I was already using it in the classroom by then, as were others. In fact, I was using journals as early as the mid- to late fifties. (Yes, I go waaaay back. I started teaching in 1951.) We didn't call it freewriting then. I always used journals as a way of helping students express themselves freely. I never "graded" them, but I did give credit for their completion. I had a couple of rules: anything they wrote, I could read. I didn't go for the clipping-pages-they-didn't-want-me-to-read practice. The journal, while

distinct from more formal writing, was still "public" in that sense. But they were, of course, very personal, as journals tend to be.

Freewriting, as it came to be known after Peter Elbow got in on the act, was somewhat different; we used it as a way of loosening up the juices, getting the hand moving over the page, regardless of what words came forth. I think this kind of freewriting is useful in the classroom in a very limited way: it is helpful for students who are not fluent, for whatever reason. Fluency is the major benefit. Once students were fluent, the ten minutes of freewriting seemed useful for very few students, the ones who were already "writers."

In my last years of teaching, I rarely used freewriting in that early Peter Elbow way. What I found much more productive was freewriting *in response to* something, generally literature, a news event, a short poem, a quotation. In addition to those quickwrites, as we called them, I also assigned reading-response journals of various kinds.

So, over thirty-five years or so of teaching, I used many different kinds of freewriting, but I always provided multiple opportunities for students to pursue their own interests in their writing.

Sarah: How has freewriting changed the field of composition, and specifically, has it changed how we think about such things as invention, voice, and style? How would you characterize any of these changes? (Generally I'm interested in anything else you might have to say about freewriting's history in the composition field.)

Fran: I do think freewriting has changed the field of teaching both composition and literature. I'm not sure that many teachers use it in the Peter Elbow way any more. But I do think most high school teachers use various models of journals/reading-response journals/quickwrites as ways of involving students in developing ideas to write about and coming to identify their own voices. As for developing style, that of course is closely tied to voice, but hard to pinpoint. I think the way I "teach" style is primarily through modeling rather than freewriting. Students try on many styles to find which ones fit best through a modeling exercise followed by various kinds of modeling extensions. I have a lot of these exercises, which are not really freewriting, but give students the development of fluency along with an understanding of style.

I can't say how extensive this practice is; certainly in the hundreds of workshops I've given, I've passed it on to many teachers. Whether they continue to find it useful is hard to say.

Sarah: Do you personally find freewriting to be a valuable classroom heuristic? Why or why not and in what contexts?

Fran: I think I've answered this; I would like to add, however, that the work I've done in graphics is correlated to what I've done with freewriting. Students draw, then write ("free" draw, then "free" write). Quickdraws followed by quickwrites generate a lot of writing. Again, I use these strategies more in relation to literature than to generating writing of students' own.

I have to add that I don't know how I got so much poetry from my students, but I did . . . from students of all levels of ability, too. There was no stopping them, once they started. Perhaps the poems began with the modeling.

Sarah: Why do you think some students love freewriting, while others seem to dread it? Are there certain kinds of students for whom freewriting is most helpful?

Fran: Most just don't know what to write about. Those who like the open time for freewriting are those who already like to write. That's why I came to tie the time to focused writing rather than freewriting. It worked for my students.

Sarah: What kind of distinctions, if any, do you make between freewriting and writing?

Fran: Very early on, during the early days of the Writing Project, I took issue with the one-way arrows that soon appeared on banners across classroom walls: titled "The Writing Process," the arrows moved from "fluency" to "form" to "correctness." Teachers taught "the" process in a linear way, from drafting to revision to editing. I always made my arrows go in both directions. The term *recursiveness* came to be honored, but I still find the old one-way "process models" on charts at the front of the room in class after class that I visit.

Sarah: Do you advocate presenting freewriting in any certain way (e.g., as an invention tool, as a way of having fun or playing with language, as the inevitable precursor to any draft)?

Fran: I love the language play although I don't necessarily tie it to freewriting. To get students started with an essay, for example, I generally offer the suggestion of clustering, drawing, freewriting . . . whatever works for each student. Of course, they need to have had the experience of all of these strategies in order to make appropriate choices. I firmly believe that we must teach students to be aware of how they learn, of how they process information, of how they generate ideas, etc. So when I present these ideas, it is always in the context of, "I want you to try this so you will know whether it will be useful for you."

Follow-up questions and answers:

Sarah: You said that you think freewriting is most useful for students who already enjoy writing and consider themselves writers. This surprised me, operating with the assumption that freewriting is a great way to help nonwriters engage in the act of writing, to play with language, get confident and comfortable, and ideally like it. This hasn't been your observation? Were you referring only to the strict no-stopping, write whatever comes to mind freewriting or even the focused freewriting to prompts?

Fran: Sarah, I think I did say that freewriting is helpful in generating fluency for students who find the act of writing difficult, whether because they are second language students or students who have not been successful in writing.

Even so, I found the focused freewriting with these students more productive in generating fluency than the strict no-stopping/no-topic method, which I used quite extensively when it first was suggested. My students did much better with a stimulus . . . whether a quotation, a poem, a newspaper article, a campus issue . . .

Sarah: Could you say any more about how freewriting may have changed English studies? Were you taught how to teach invention to your students when you entered the field in the fifties? I have these two hypotheses at work about how it was before freewriting. One is that more logical methods of invention were taught, like Aristotle's topics, and so freewriting was a huge shift—suddenly the writer is a source of knowledge and creativity is valued as much as or more than logic. The other is that no invention strategies were explicitly taught—a student was given a subject and proceeded blindly from there. Does either hypothesis have any truth to it or are they stereotypical myths?

Fran: Preparation for teaching composition in the fifties was practically nonexistent. As a new teacher, all I had to go on was how I had been taught. For me, that meant a very specific assignment, a set number of pages or words. I introduced the journal simply because I believed it to be a useful way of getting ideas, finding out what one might want to write about, etc. I had no models for this early on. In fact, I had no models for anything my first few years of teaching (in Ohio). English in those days meant grammar and literature, with essays attached to the literature study. For some reason, I was assigned the writing of a sonnet in my senior year, and I had been writing poetry by myself, showing it to no one, of course. I don't know how that came about. I went to a very academic public high school, so my "training" in grammar was excessive. I still enjoy being the grammar maven when I can get away with it.

I'm not sure how I came to be so involved in teaching composition, actually trying to teach it rather than assign it. I think it stemmed from my own interest in writing. I always had my students writing reams of poetry as well as other kinds of writing—the essays, of course, but also memoir and story. My "reluctant" writers became poets. I find that the writing of poetry is a powerful way of helping these students overcome the "essay failure" they have experienced in school.

It was a great joy to me to find the surge of interest in teaching composition, which for me became evident in the mid- to late sixties. I was influenced by James Moffett, of course, and then by my work with the Writing Project.

Sarah: How is the modern classroom functioning differently from the days before freewriting?

Fran: There is just no comparison between many classrooms today and those of the fifties. I will say, however, that some teachers could be teaching at my old school still. I don't think all English teachers are practicing effective teaching of composition, by any means. But more are than are not. Some of the current practices are badly skewed by writing "programs" that distort the ideas of how writers write, forcing kids into stereotypical formulas that are far removed from the ideas of Elbow, Moffett, Janet Emig, etc.

I have seen very effective writing workshop elementary classrooms. I haven't seen many at the high school level. That doesn't mean they don't exist; I just haven't seen them.

An aside: One of the trends I see that is very prevalent is teaching writing by beginning with rubrics for various genres, then teaching students to write within the scope of the rubric. This is a difficult situation for me as I do talk and write about features of different genres, but I hope to help teachers teach the genres by using the inductive method of having students read widely, study features, then incorporate these features into their own writing. Class-generated rubrics name and elaborate on the features they have noticed as being typical of a particular genre. The work with rubrics, then, helps students become self-assessors.

So, how does freewriting (or focused freewriting) enter into the prewriting phase of writing in different genres? Actually, I don't even like the term "prewriting" any more, since what I used to call prewriting is simply one phase of writing, and, as I said before, it is recursive. I may stop at any point and do some reflective generating of ideas.

As you see, what I am doing now is simply reflecting on some of your questions in a very freewheeling way. I hope this will be of some use to you.

II Rethinking Genre

*A body of writing may take any
   of a thousand forms,
   and there is no one right way to measure.*

   The Art of Writing: Lu Chi's Wen Fu, "Catalog of Genres"

*Knowledge of genres is essential to reading and writing, making reading
comprehensible and writing possible.*

Charles Cooper

Modes of writing, often referred to as genres, arise out of the relationships among purpose, audience, subject, and form. We look here at the features of specific genres not as frameworks for composing but as artifacts. Genres can be seen as the end products of writing, pieces that possess, to one degree or another, features that help us see them as belonging to a cultural category—stories or reports or interpretations. This approach acknowledges that one genre may fold into another, that a persuasive piece may be filled with narratives, that reflection is part of most kinds of writing. This distinction, describing genres as end products rather than templates, may seem a fine point, but for the writing teacher it is crucial that we use genre knowledge as a way of looking at how writers can learn to make decisions based on purpose. Overlapping features of genres become key strategies—narrating, describing, explaining, persuading, reflecting, interpreting, analyzing, investigating, evaluating—as they are used across genres in papers ranging from essay to report, from memoir to poem.

As important as it is to acknowledge writing that doesn't fit easily into kinds of writing with names and predictable features, it is equally important to help writers see how genre knowledge can play a critical role in their crafting and revising. With this approach, we see the act of writing as having recursive rather than linear dimensions, as we deal with the writer's stance in relation to text and acknowledge movement in that stance.

Charles Cooper, in an article titled "What We Know about Genres," writes, "Written genres appear inevitably, predictably, in any literate society or culture. They are not imposed from above by an elite, nor are they isolated from social interactions and the need to communicate. Members of a society recognize its genres, benefit from them, and value them. Knowledge of genres is essential to reading and writing, making reading comprehensible and writing possible" (25).

The field of genre studies often includes the whole range of literate behaviors—written, oral, visual, musical—as genres, each with its own sphere of purposes, audiences, text (or nontext) structures, patterns of grammar, typical vocabulary, community expectations, assumed background knowledge, and so on. Some teacher-researchers are exploring having students deconstruct texts to elicit the generic features.

The genres we deal with in this book describe the kinds of writing most often taught in middle and high schools. We do not mean to imply that these are the only genres that should be taught or that they should be taught in isolation. Indeed, we acknowledge and support the blending of genres as appropriate for a particular purpose determined by students or by teachers.

Genre and Purpose: Eliciting Generic Features

In order to familiarize students with the more obvious features of a genre they are likely to read and to write, we suggest setting up a protocol for students to elicit generic features from a model, using books and articles in the classroom or school library. Here is one approach to this activity:

Have on hand magazines, books of essays, poems, reports, etc.

- Before reading, ask the question "What are some of the purposes people have for writing?" Place these horizontally, in one row, on the board.

- Have students, working in pairs, browse through as many pieces as they can in fifteen or twenty minutes. For each piece that they read, have them answer the question "What seems to be the purpose of this piece of writing?"

- Next have them, still in pairs, assemble at least three titles that seem to share a purpose.

- Studying these selected pieces, students should then elicit and record the shared characteristics or features of the pieces that had a common purpose.

Using the various purposes listed on the board, students should write down characteristics they found in their focused browsing. When several groups study texts with common purposes, have them note similarities and differences in their lists of features. They can then update their own lists to keep in their notebooks.

This activity will serve as a starting point for a discussion of purposes in writing. We suggest that you repeat this activity with preselected texts as you introduce different genres to the class.

Guides to Teaching Specific Genres

Chapters 3 through 7 present guides to teaching these genres: interpretation, persuasion, evaluation, reflection, and memoir. Each guide will have these sections:

- Introduction to the genre
- Features of the genre
- Teaching activities for the genre
- Suggestions for assessment
- Sample of student work

Note: As we present different genres in this book, we will offer different kinds of rubrics or other assessment strategies.

Background Information on Genre Study

There are three major traditions of genre research, each having implications for how we teach writing. I am indebted to Greta Volmer from Sonoma State University and a team of Bay Area Writing Project teacher-researchers for presenting these ideas to a group of interested Writing Project consultants. As this was an oral presentation, I take responsibility for any deviation from their intent.

- The Applied Linguistics Approach defines *genre* as "communicative events" characterized by "communicative purposes" and various patterns of structure, style, content, and intended audience. This tradition stresses the importance of a student's apprenticeship in a new discourse community and has particular concerns for teachers of second language learners.
- The North American New Rhetoric Approach defines genre as "social action" in an institutional context. Studies in this tradition are concerned primarily with university academic writing. By extension, we can apply the questions posed by this tradition to our upper-level honors and Advanced Placement

courses in high schools. Here a basic question is whether genre knowledge can or should be explicitly taught or whether it is simply acquired through socialization into a particular disciplinary community.

- The Australian School Approach is more focused on primary and secondary school writing and the nonprofessional work world, especially with linguistic/cultural minorities and adult ESL populations. The key question for these researchers has been "How can we best teach students, especially those who are marginalized linguistically and culturally, the 'powerful' genres they need to succeed in school and participate fully in their communities?"

For a comprehensive treatment—an informative article as well as other genre-related materials—we suggest, among the rich sources of such material on the Web, Daniel Chandler's "Introduction to Genre Theory" on his Web site.

3 Interpretation

Interpretation as a kind of writing has a long history: it is a basic human impulse to take a text, an event, or a phenomenon and try to explain its meaning in one's own words. Beyond enhancing self-knowledge, interpretation may convey one's insights to another. To make that leap in writing, from one mind to another, a writer must name the subject to be interpreted and provide a context for interpretation. The writer must then make claims about his or her understanding of the subject and provide some kind of support for those claims.

Since interpretation is central to many thinking behaviors, interpretive writing has much in common with other types of writing: from *memoir*, students bring narrative examples with specific, telling details to elaborate the claims of interpretation; from *persuasion*, the ability to develop criteria and present evidence; from *reflection*, the awareness of the importance of spinning an idea out, moving from the personal to the general. These strategies central to other kinds of writing become ancillary in the interpretive essay, where the primary object is to make meaning of a text, an event, or a person's behavior.

Features of an Interpretation Essay

Writers of interpretive essays must make claims about their understanding of the meaning of an event, a phenomenon, or a work of literature or art, and support these claims. While different writers may make different claims about the same subject, the effectiveness of the interpretation depends largely on the strength and convincing presentation of the support provided for the initial claims.

The following characteristics are common to interpretive essays: point of departure, interpretive claim(s), support, and stance.

- Point of Departure: To focus the interpretation effectively, the writer establishes a point of departure for the essay. The writer introduces the subject, forecasts the essay's intent, and provides adequate context for the reader. Although the amount of contextual background varies, depending on the writer's assessment of the intended reader, context should not dominate the essay.

- Interpretive Claim(s): Within the framework of the context, the writer presents and develops interpretive claims, which, together with their support, create the central focus of the essay.

- Support: The writer's task throughout the essay is to provide support in arguing for these claims by introducing personal experience, prior knowledge, related readings, and textual evidence, often including direct quotations. Elaboration of and support for the interpretive claims provide the bulk of most interpretive essays.

- Stance: To persuade readers that the interpretation is reasonable and valid, the writer takes a strong, consistent stance and maintains it. The organization of the essay helps the reader perceive the writer's position.

A Cautionary Note: During the process of writing an interpretive essay, a reader often develops new insights about the meaning of the subject. In a first draft of an interpretive essay, the reader/writer may discover that his or her original claims are no longer valid. These changes in understanding will help determine the course of subsequent revisions, but an early draft should not be criticized for failure to maintain a position on interpretive claims.

Teaching the Interpretive Essay

I: Getting Started: "What Do You Make of It?"

Every time we use Louise Rosenblatt's provocative starter question "What do you make of it?" after the reading of a text, we stimulate interpretive thinking. The first time you use it, you may expect confused silence. Let the silence hold, however, and you will be surprised at the quality of comments that students begin to offer. This question, thrown out for small-group discussion or for a journal entry before discussion, is an excellent way to initiate the kind of thinking that leads to good interpretive writing. It forces the burden of making meaning onto the thinker/writer rather than onto the teacher/expert or other secondary source.

The dialectical or dual-entry journal is a tool that is invaluable for reader/writers who are learning to trust their own interpretations. The basic instructions are simple:

> Instructions for the Dual-Entry Journal
>
> 1. Draw a line down the center of the page.
> 2. On the left side, copy quotations from the text. You might select passages that intrigue you for various reasons: you may have had similar experiences or feelings; the passage may be confusing; you may disagree with the ideas expressed; you may want to explore an idea in your own words.

3. On the right side of the page, write your response to each passage you recorded. You might address such topics as these:

- what you think about this character's behavior
- what other poem/book/film/play this reminds you of
- what the passage might mean
- an experience of your own that is like that recounted in the passage
- what surprised you about this event/action
- what confused you about the passage
- what might happen next
- what stopped you at this point

II: Suggested Interpretation Essay Assignments in Various Disciplines

While the classroom writing assignments suggested here may seem like the traditional, whole-class assignments, they assume a full range of teaching strategies—personal journals, dialectical journals, paralogues, graphic interpretations of the metaphorical meanings of a work, group discussion—as part of the interpretive process. Students who have had experience in the range of interpretive experiences will be able to handle writing essays in testing situations with confidence.

English: Author Study, Incorporating an Interpretation Essay

In preparing to write an interpretive essay on some aspect of a single novelist's work, students engage in the following steps:

- Select an author (a student may select from the teacher's list or have an individual choice approved, but each student must find at least one other student to read the same author).
- Read at least three of the author's novels, keeping a dialectical journal during the reading.
- Get together with the other people in the class who have read this author for their study.
- After discussion of the works read, focus on dominant themes, ideas, symbols, kinds of characters, typical settings, etc., common to this author's work.
- Prepare a group graphic display dealing with whatever the group feels is most significant about this author's work. The graphic may include both visual and verbal ingredients. (See the appendix for the standard for and definitions of visual literacy and graphic maps.)

- Using the graphic and whatever other ideas the group has, present their author to the class. (Some groups may design author interviews, dramatize scenes, portion out sections for separate student presentations, etc.) Follow the presentation with class discussion.

- Write an extended piece in the style of the author. (Note: See Chapter 9, "Learning Writing Strategies through Modeling," for a further explanation of this assignment.)

As a final step in the author-study project, each student writes an interpretive essay on some aspect of the author's work. Another possibility is an optional assignment involving film: After students have read a novel and seen a film based on that novel, ask groups to compare the two works with regard to plot and character motivation. After discussion of the various findings of different groups, ask students to write an interpretive essay on some aspect of the work that they found treated differently in the two media. (Examples of readily available film/novel combinations include William Golding's *Lord of the Flies,* Harper Lee's *To Kill a Mockingbird,* John Steinbeck's *Cannery Row* and *East of Eden,* Charles Dickens's *Great Expectations,* and John Knowles's *A Separate Peace.*)

History/Social Studies

In a social studies class, students may conduct an independent study of the Vietnam War and its effects on the country then and now. Students may

- read novels or firsthand accounts of the war;
- read journals and journalistic accounts of the pacifists who evaded the draft;
- study the effect of the Vietnam Veterans Memorial on families of soldiers killed in the war. One or more students, perhaps, might visit the memorial in honor of a relative.

Each student, if possible, conducts an interview with someone who was affected by the Vietnam War. After sharing their individual work in discussion groups and preparing their data—charts, graphics, pictures—each student writes an interpretive essay on some aspect of the effect of the Vietnam War on a person, a group, or the entire country.

Science

During a laboratory experiment, students keep notes and drawings. Afterwards, they interpret their findings, based on a careful analysis of their notes.

Mathematics

Students may interpret a graph or chart. For example, students may interpret a graph or chart showing the statistics on the number of eighteen-year-olds voting in the national election. They may interpret a graph or chart showing the breakdown of expenses for a first-year college student in a two-year college, a state university, and a private college or university. For these interpretations, students would need to find a focus for their theses, make claims for their interpretations, and use support directly from the charts or graphs.

III: Response, Revision, and Editing

The peer-response revision process presents a rich, thorough format for students to use in helping one another revise their papers. There are many possible formats for response/revision. Many teachers find that modeling response groups (having a small, trained group model for the entire class) is a useful way to introduce groups. Students need to learn how to read their papers aloud to others and to help guide the discussion so that they get real help with revision.

After students have completed their final drafts, you may want to have them write a journal entry assessing their revision processes, describing the changes they made from their first drafts and thinking about the total writing process.

Deep Editing and Surface Editing

Editing is not an inborn talent. It takes teaching, as do the other aspects of writing. While editing or proofreading is the final step before publication, that does not imply that the writer should not be aware of and correcting errors along the way. The way a writer rephrases an idea may involve a more complicated or a simpler sentence structure; as writers make such changes, they should be aware of the need for changes in punctuation or grammar.

That said, time should be allotted for the final surface editing. This is the time to proofread work and correct any spelling, punctuation, or grammatical errors that remain. This revision will probably be the finished product; the way the writers present their papers says a lot about them as writers and about their concern for their readers.

One Process for Analyzing an Interpretive Essay

Have students work with a writing partner on response and revision. You might use some of the questions in the peer-response guide below to guide their thinking. The writer of the paper should be clear that the final decisions are the writer's. Remember that the writer is the *author* of the paper and that gives *authority*. But ask students to consider their partner's responses very carefully; it is important to know how readers respond to their writing.

For revising it's very helpful if students read their words aloud. We strongly recommend that students read the draft aloud to a partner or group and/or have someone read it aloud to them. As they hear their words, they may identify awkward sentences or unclear ideas. They should use their own knowledge plus that of their response partners to revise their papers.

Peer-Response Guide: Directions to Students:
Read your partner's draft and write your responses to the following requests. Refer to specific page numbers, paragraphs, and lines when you need to point out a particular place in your partner's paper.

- Paraphrase the writer's thesis or central idea. Is the first paragraph clear or does it sound uncertain? Explain.
- If necessary, how can the writer improve the beginning?
- List the claims the writer makes; check to see whether the claims relate to the thesis.
- Note the supporting reasons; check whether the evidence illustrates each reason. Does the student have some direct quotations as proof from the text? Is the support sufficiently detailed? If not, indicate where the writer needs to elaborate.
- Is there too much summary or too little analysis? Explain and make suggestions as to how the writer might improve the balance.
- Note passages that are particularly effective—surprising ideas, memorable phrases, or striking images.
- If you find any places that are difficult to understand or need transitions, mark these passages.
- Read the concluding paragraph(s). The conclusion does not simply summarize—it should offer additional insights. Tell the writer your views on the conclusion and how it might be strengthened if it needs to be.

The Finished Paper

Now that most of our students are computer-literate, we may laugh at the old admonition to write "in ink, on one side of the paper, and watch the margins," but we still need to set standards for the presentation of final copies of major papers. Students need to know the parameters, including the date a paper is due, in ample time to meet the deadline. They need to know the consequences of late papers, and the other rituals of your particular classroom structure.

The following interpretive essay was written by Desmond Chin when he was a junior.

The World of Petals
by Desmond Chin
Teacher: Joan Brown

The world of F. Scott Fitzgerald's *The Great Gatsby* is a flower consisting of a center and a corolla of petals. The flower itself forms a world that, having survived a war, was now disillusioned and complacent about traditional values and was probing for new codes of morals and understanding. Aspiring flappers and their ardent wooers, many of whom affected an air of bewildered abandonment toward life, came to feed on the nectar, which the flower produced. Within this flower was a nucleus, New York, which linked the other three petals together: East Egg, West Egg, and the Valley of Ashes. Together, the nucleus and the corolla formed the East, the world in which Fitzgerald's characters lived; however, each petal and nucleus possessed characteristics of its own kind and was a world separate from the other parts of the flower, influencing the actions of the characters.

Both the East Egg and the West Egg were connected to each other, "identical in contour and separated only by a courtesy bay"; however, they were dissimilar ". . . in every particular except shape and size." East Egg represented the traditional, established community with its "white palaces." It was in this proper, well-mannered part of the town where light-headed women sat in enormous couches and ". . . were buoyed up as though upon an anchored balloon." East Egg was a place of confinement and masks. People did not walk around in comfortable pajamas and tennis shoes. Instead, three-piece suits were worn all day and women such as Daisy and Jordan hobbled along with three-inch heels and were ". . . like silver idols weighing down their own white dresses against the singing breeze of the fans." When asked to stand they would simply reply, "We can't move." Tom Buchanan, who had an affair with Myrtle Wilson, never mentioned his relationship with Myrtle in East Egg. He masked his affair and only ". . . turned up in popular restaurants with her" once he had safely stepped across the egg shell.

Unlike the austere, snub-nosed society of East Egg, West Egg was Gatsby's creation to lure his object into his arms. It saw the birth, or perhaps the rebirth of a relationship between Gatsby and Daisy. West Egg served as a womb for Gatsby, which kept him comfortable yet dormant until "he came alive . . . delivered suddenly from the womb of his purposeless splendor." West Egg was devoted entirely to Daisy. Gatsby had bought his West Egg house ". . . so that Daisy would be just across the bay." Without her, the West portion of the egg would serve no purpose. The "wild rout" parties which were held almost every night served only to attract Daisy from her green light in East Egg to the blazing lights of West Egg. The parties themselves were purposeless, a potpourri of "nobodies" who were thrown together to form ". . . a burst of chatter." Fitzgerald tells us that, "People were not invited—they went there" just to have fun and to be included in the frolic." It was in West Egg where there were "enthusiastic meetings between women who never knew each other's names." It was the one place where the so-called Hornbeams and the Willie Voltairs from East Egg paired up with the void Fausting O'Brien or Ardita Fitz-Peters. "All these people came to Gatsby's house in the summer" with no real purpose except to perhaps join the bandwagon of social life. In fact, "Sometimes they came and went without having met Gatsby at all, came for the party with a simplicity of heart that was its own ticket of admission." Every night, these people came and went and the next night they would come again and leave at the same time. The party-goers resembled crates of oranges and lemons that arrived at Gatsby's door every Monday and ". . . left his back door in a pyramid of pulpless halves," having gone through a "machine in the kitchen which could extract the juice . . . in half an hour if a little button was pressed two hundred times." Thus, West Egg represented the mechanistic manner in which humans run their lives, being continuously squeezed by one machine after the other, and always going through doors labeled "entrances" and "exits" because they had no direction to their lives.

Contrary to the wild parties, the Valley of Ashes was a "gray land" covered with "spasms of black dust which drift endlessly over it." It represented the Greek god Hades' dominion where "ashes grow like wheat into ridges and hills and grotesque gardens," and where Hades watched over the inhabitants and the land. In this case, Hades is the eyes of Doctor T. J. Eckleburg that "brood on over the solemn dumping ground" and keep watch over all activity. Just as the underworld was bounded by the river Styx, there was also a "small foul river" which bounded the Valley of Ashes. Like spirits roaming the land, people and things in the valley are colored gray and were bounded by a film of ash. There was a "gray, scrawny Italian child . . . setting torpedoes in a row along the railroad track," a "line of gray cars crawling along an invisible track," and "ash-gray men" who would "swarm up with leaden spades and stir up an impenetrable cloud."

New York on the other hand, was the playground society. It was the one place that connected East Egg, West Egg, and the

Valley of Ashes, and all the characters with the exception of Wilson used it as an escape hatch from their own petals of society. When Tom and Myrtle wanted to meet and hold hands, they "went up together to New York," and when Nick, Jordan, Daisy, Gatsby, and Tom wanted to get away from the heat and have fun, they "went into town." New York attracted these people because it was the center of society. It was a place where "anything went"—both good and bad. People removed their masks and revealed their true selves, such as Myrtle, whose ". . . intense vitality that had not been so remarkable in the garage, was converted into impressive hauteur." It was also in New York where intensive gambling and fraud played the main actors on the stage. It was the home of Meyer Wolfsheim who, with his "gonnegtion" was a gambler who fixed the World Series in 1919 and who constantly turned ". . . to inspect the people directly behind," hoping that no one was following him. New York was also the place for hard liquor, perhaps representing the toughness and vigor of the city. Whenever Nick, Tom, Daisy, Myrtle, etc. were in New York, they would "unroll the bottle of whiskey," whereas in East Egg or West Egg, they would clink champagne glasses.

New York, as well as the other settings, sustained the lives of the characters and nourished their appetite for excitement and pleasure. However, when the umbilical cords of Gatsby, Wilson, and Myrtle were severed, the connections that had linked all the characters together had been broken and the flower with its corolla and nucleus began to fold. Daisy no longer had a life with Gatsby; nor could Myrtle and Wilson spend time away from the Valley of Ashes. Death had claimed those three characters, and the remaining characters, finding the nectar no longer sweet, flew away from the flower. Nick went back to the Mid-West; Jordan became engaged to another man, and Daisy and Tom had gone away and taken baggage with them. The four settings—East Egg, West Egg, New York, and the Valley of Ashes—still retained their own unique characteristics, but the characters themselves, through events and character interaction, changed through the book, and as a result, the settings no longer complemented them. Thus the flower, representing the settings, withdrew, while the characters traveled their own paths and "beat on," like "boats against the current," following their own drift to wherever it might lead them.

Assessing the Interpretive Essay

Following is a four-point interpretive essay rubric. Intended to be used to evaluate the quality of the interpretation of a text as well as the quality of the writing itself, this rubric can be considered both a reading and a writing rubric. Although there are more sophisticated reading rubrics than this one, it provides a useful holistic evaluation for a classroom or a department.

Four-Point Interpretation Essay Rubric

4	The essay ■ demonstrates a thorough grasp of the text; ■ addresses all parts of the writing task; ■ provides a meaningful thesis and maintains a consistent tone and focus; ■ illustrates a purposeful control of organization; ■ thoughtfully supports the thesis and main ideas with specific details and examples from the text and from personal knowledge and experience; ■ uses language with precision to convey ideas; often inventive in use of analogies; and ■ contains few, if any, errors in the conventions of the English language. (Errors are generally first-draft in nature.)
3	The essay ■ demonstrates a comprehensive grasp of the text; ■ addresses all parts of the writing task; ■ provides a thesis and maintains a consistent tone and focus; ■ illustrates a control of organization; ■ supports the thesis and main ideas with details and examples from the text and generally from personal knowledge and experience; ■ uses language that conveys meaning clearly; and ■ may contain some errors in the conventions of the English language, but errors do not interfere with the reader's understanding of the essay.
2	The essay ■ demonstrates a limited comprehension of the text; ■ addresses only parts of the writing task; ■ may provide a thesis; may present an inconsistent tone and focus; ■ illustrates little, if any, control of organization; ■ may support the thesis and main ideas with limited, if any, details and/or examples from the text or personal knowledge; ■ uses basic, predictable language; and ■ usually contains a number of errors in the conventions of the English language. Errors may interfere with the reader's understanding of the essay.
1	The essay may be too short to evaluate, or it ■ demonstrates little, if any, overall grasp of the text; ■ may provide a weak, if any, thesis; fails to maintain a focus; ■ illustrates little or no control of organization; ■ fails to support ideas with details and/or examples; ■ uses limited vocabulary; and ■ contains serious errors in the conventions of the English language. Errors interfere with the reader's understanding of the essay.
not scorable	Essay may be blank, off-topic, written in a language other than English, illegible, or unintelligible.

Appendix: Standard for Visual Literacy

Students will create and explain conceptual graphic representations of characters, symbols, and ideas in literary works as they visualize and articulate their own symbolic understandings of texts.

Elaboration

A *graphic* is a visual construct using lines, words, and color in a symbolic way to create a coherent conceptual design. It presents a unifying symbol or related set of symbols arising from a piece of literature. The graphic symbol may be drawn from the text itself (the pig's head in *Lord of the Flies*, the urn in Keats's "Ode on a Grecian Urn") or it may evolve from metaphor making (a bat to represent Teiresias, signifying outward blindness but inward seeing). In some graphics, the design may point to symbols rather than depict them overtly, as in lines suggesting spiderwebs or geometric demarcations suggesting beehive cells.

The graphic uses color or lack of color with intent. Color may be used symbolically or it may be used to organize aspects of the graphic. Black-and-white graphics may be used in the Japanese sense of Notan (echoed in the work of M. C. Escher) to convey positive and negative space or emotion.

Literary graphics as study aids frequently incorporate quotations from the text. For those graphics intended to be used as maps for writing papers, it is important for the graphic artist to include the textual reference for the quotation. Quotations are often used artistically to support the visual construct.

Through the production of graphics, students experience four critical learning functions—observing, analyzing, imaging, and feeling—as they interact with the texts they are reading and the essays, articles, stories, and poems they are writing.

They learn to develop their ways of learning in three significant ways. They learn:

1. to activate the powers of imagery, detail, symbol, and design as they read and write;
2. to incorporate close observation, personal association, analysis, and metaphor in reading and writing; and
3. to stimulate the long-term memory through the integration of both visual and verbal approaches.

Graphic strategies address the needs of the full range of students, including

1. students who are new to this country and just learning its language as well as its customs;

2. students who are labeled "learning disabled" in our primarily verbal/analytical schools; such students may be among those whose dominant learning mode is visual-spatial;

3. students labeled culturally "deprived" when they are unfamiliar with the dominant culture of the schoolroom, but rich in their own ethnic cultures; and

4. the academically gifted, who either drop out from boredom or learn to play the competitive, limiting "game" of *school.*

For extensive use of graphics in teaching composition and literature, see *Drawing Your Own Conclusions: Graphic Strategies in Reading, Writing, and Thinking,* by Fran Claggett with Joan Brown.

4 Persuasion

Joan Brown

The measure of a master is his success in bringing all men round to his opinion twenty years later.

Ralph Waldo Emerson

The term *persuasive* is an umbrella-term, encompassing a variety of writing types; and each of those types in turn includes many different kinds of writing. For example, editorials, political speeches, letters of complaint and/or request, trial lawyers' closing arguments, and essays that advocate a particular side of an issue are all types of argumentation. Critiques, employee evaluations, and restaurant, movie, and book reviews are also among the many different kinds of evaluation; and problem-solution papers, essays explaining what something might mean or speculating about causes or effects, papers explaining a particular view of a character or situation, or papers explaining how and/or why something works as it does are all kinds of persuasion.[1]

Features of Persuasive Writing

Though the specific task will differ and the structure and details will vary according to the given situation, the writer's goal in a persuasive essay is always to influence readers, to get readers to agree with the writer's opinion, or at least to convince readers that the opinion is worth serious consideration even if in the end they still don't agree with it. And because this goal is constant, all persuasive writing—whether the task is to write an advertisement or a position paper, a problem-solution paper or an essay exam—has the same components:

- A situation or issue
- A claim or arguable opinion about that issue
- Plausible reasons and relevant evidence that illustrate and support that claim
- Acknowledgment and consideration of other possible views
- An ongoing explanation of why, having seriously considered these opposing opinions, the writer stands by his or her own view and encourages readers to agree

Teaching the Persuasive Essay

Most of us are quick to offer opinions about a myriad of subjects; however, an opinion is not persuasive unless it is bolstered by facts and reasons that develop and support it. In this section we focus on students' own natural persuasiveness, on the prevalence of persuasion around them, and on the techniques and strategies that others use both to persuade and to manipulate them.

What Persuades?

1. Have students list times during the last week that they encountered persuasion—times when either someone tried to persuade them in some way, or they tried to persuade someone else in some way.

2. Create the following chart on the board and generate a list of different kinds of persuasion and of techniques that people use to persuade. Help students see beyond the obvious, to recognize as persuasive such things as advertisements (the backs of cereal boxes as well as radio and TV ads), asking for a favor of a friend or parent, phone solicitations, job applications, a movie recommendation by a friend, music lyrics, articles and/or editorials in newspapers and magazines, proposals, etc.

Here is a sample chart that might emerge from this activity:

What	Who	How	Results
Change curfew time	mother	begged	said no
Turn in homework late	teacher	gave excuses	okay
Buy a product	salesperson—ad	made promises	didn't do it
Bathe dog	sister	threatened	did it
Borrow new sweater	friend	offered to loan new shirt	wore sweater to movie

You might mention that some types of persuasion—threatening, begging, whining, crying, throwing tantrums, holding your breath until you turn blue in the face—are rather immature and not worthy of consideration, even if they do sometimes work.

3. Ask students to write brief responses to each of the following aspects of persuasion:

- Observe it: What can persuasion do?

(Get you to take action: buy something, join a group, give money, behave a certain way; get you to think or believe something: support a cause, change an idea, etc.)

- Classify it: What kinds are there? What varieties or forms does it come in?
  (Advertisements, job or school applications, editorials, threats, proposals, policy memos, insurance claims, etc.)

- Analyze it: What is persuasion made of? How is it done? What are the parts? What does it take to persuade you of something?
  (Opinions, reasons, examples, name-dropping of others who agree, bribes, promises, etc.)

- Defend it: What's good about persuasion?
  (Can make you aware of other points of view; can introduce you to a new idea, etc.)

- Trash it: What's bad about persuasion?
  (Can manipulate you—if you let it.)

- Relate to it: What kinds of persuasion do you know about? What persuasive techniques? What persuades you?

- Define it: What *is* persuasive? What *isn't* persuasive?

4. Have students share their responses in small groups or with partners, adding to and clarifying their initial responses. Work toward eliciting ideas such as the following:

- A broad definition such as: *Persuasion is influencing someone or trying to get someone to think, believe, or act in a particular way. It is, in effect, a request, implicit or explicit, that someone believe or act in a given way.*

- A starter-list of *kinds or types* of persuasion—of where we encounter it or engage in it ourselves: *in advertisements, job applications, junk mail, conversations with family members, movie or restaurant reviews, etc.*

- A starter-list of *techniques:* explorations of the ways such influencing can be done: *through emotional appeal; through logical reasoning; through threats; through outright lies.*

When to Persuade

Explain to students that in all writing, as is true in any expressive act, a writer's purpose will determine the process he or she chooses to use, and that process will shape the product that the writer produces. For example, they would not use primarily storytelling techniques if their purpose were to explain how to change a tire (unless they were writing a children's book). They would not use primarily persuasive techniques if the assignment were to dispatch information in a research report. It is important therefore for students to recognize *when* an assignment is calling for persuasion; and it is equally important for them to recognize the specific reason for which they are using it.

Reinforce the point made earlier that if the writer's primary purpose is to influence readers, to convince readers to seriously consider his or her point of view about an issue, he or she will write persuasion. In short, persuasion says to its audience, "This is what I think, and this is why I think it;" or "This is what you should do and this is why you should do it."

Discuss the following points:

- Persuasion assumes the need to give an opinion, to point something out, to broaden reader awareness, or to change someone's mind. It presents an issue, a situation, or an opinion that reasonable, well-educated people can and do view differently; and it assumes that, given rational and relevant evidence and arguments, the audience might be influenced to agree with the writer or at least to consider and acknowledge the writer's point of view.
- Persuasion is unnecessary when there is already widespread agreement about an issue or situation.
- Persuasion is inappropriate when questions allow for only one correct answer.

Discuss the various reasons that writers might have for wanting to influence readers, noting that the specific reason will determine the kind of persuasive essay that the writer will produce. The most common types of persuasive essays are the *argumentative essay,* the *evaluation essay* or *critique,* and the *interpretive essay.* (Note that interpretation, a kind of persuasion, is treated as a separate genre in this book because of the pervasiveness of its use in the high school curriculum. See Chapter 3.)

Facts, Opinions, and Claims

Like most writing, persuasion is based on the opinion of the writer; however, because not all opinions are immediately arguable, it is good to spend a little time helping students distinguish between personal opinions, facts, and claims or arguable opinions before moving into reading and writing persuasive essays. Here is a suggested procedure:

1. Open this lesson by asking students to brainstorm a list of opinions, ideas, and/or questions about homework. They might generate such statements as these:

- Teachers give way too much homework.

- No one learns anything from doing homework.
- I don't see why we have to do homework.
- Homework is a waste of time.
- Lots of the time the parents do students' homework for them.
- Students in other countries do less homework than we do.
- I spend more time doing homework than anything else.
- There should be a law limiting the amount of homework teachers can give.

2. Ask students to hold those thoughts for a few minutes, and write the following statements on the board:

- The weekend curfews cities place on teenagers are unrealistic.
- Cities should eliminate weekend curfews for teenagers.

Now initiate a discussion about the difference between an *opinion* and a *position*. Explain that a position takes an arguable stand on an issue. Help students see that, although both of these statements are opinions, only the second statement takes a position on an issue. Emphasize that almost all persuasive writing is based on the opinion of the writer; however, not all opinions are arguable. It is important that students understand and recognize the kinds of claims that are arguable.

3. Spend a little time having students look up and discuss the definitions of claims, facts, and personal opinions. Then have students identify each of their statements about homework as you discuss the differences among these terms.

From Personal Opinion to Arguable Claim

1. Open by reviewing the definition for an arguable claim:

- A claim states the writer's position on an arguable issue.

Explain that personal opinions and even facts can sometimes be transformed into claims simply by rewording them so they present an arguable position on a subject.

2. Put the following statement on the board, and be sure students recognize it as a personal opinion, unarguable as it stands:

- Eight o'clock classes are torture.

Have students reword this statement to assert a position on the issue of eight o'clock classes, rather than a personal opinion. For example, they might change the statement to read:

- Schools should provide alternatives to eight o'clock classes.

Now the statement no longer relies solely on one person's personal and subjective feelings, memories, or preferences for support, and as such it becomes an arguable claim.

3. Now put the following two statements on the board:

    - Thanksgiving is celebrated on the last Thursday in November.
    - The sun is ninety-three million miles from the earth.

Explain that although both of these are statements of fact, only the second is "clad in stone." The first, though currently standing as fact, could be changed (and, in fact was changed during the presidency of Franklin D. Roosevelt) and therefore presents an opportunity for argument. It might, for instance, be reworded to say: "We should celebrate Thanksgiving on the last Friday in November rather than on the last Thursday." Now it presents an arguable position, and can stand as a claim.

The statement about the sun, however, cannot be reworded into a claim, since it presents a fact that is simply unchangeable.

Appealing to the Audience

Explain that once they have identified the issues and determined what they think about them, it's time to decide to word their appeals to persuade their audience to their position.

Discuss ways of appealing to people persuasively. After some time, check to see whether students have come up with these three basic methods of appeal: *emotional, ethical,* and *logical.* Persuasive writers use these appeals very purposefully both in deciding which reasons for their claims will most effectively influence their audience, and in choosing evidence that will most effectively support those reasons.

Clarify these ways of appealing through discussion:

- Emotional appeals play to the feelings or emotions of the audience. Most commonly, writers appeal to self-interest, fear, pity, humor, sympathy, affection, and/or pride.
- Ethical appeals play to the values or principles of the audience. There are certain values that most people believe in—fairness, honesty, freedom, loyalty, patriotism, helping the less fortunate, education, kindness to animals, respect for the elderly, and so on. In using ethical appeals writers may use any one of these values to support their position. Such arguments can be extremely persuasive.
- Logical appeals are directed to rational argument and the use

of facts. They engage the reader's need for consistency and organized thought.

Point out that each of these appeals can be used either persuasively or manipulatively to influence audiences, and it falls to audiences to be both deliberate and selective in determining what claims, what reasons, and what evidence they will accept.

Now ask students, "Generally, what kinds of reasons can we give people to convince them to agree with us or to do what we want them to do? Why, for example, should you stay in school right now?" You might get such responses as:

- "You'll get a better job and have a better life."
- "It's the right thing to do. To be a responsible citizen in the twenty-first century you need an education."
- "It's the sensible thing to do. As a young, single person you are unencumbered by the emotional and financial responsibilities of building a career and supporting a family so you can focus your time and your energy on completing your education."

Discuss the fact that most of us are interested in things and ideas that we believe will benefit us. Most people, for instance, want a comfortable, contented life for themselves and their families; and most people would agree with proposals and opinions that foster positive values such as fairness, responsibility, honesty, and kindness.

This means that every single step of the way, persuasive writers need to be focused on three things:

- Who's my audience? To whom am I talking?
- What's my claim? What idea, opinion, and/or proposal am I "selling?"
- Why should my audience "buy?" What's in it for them? How will they benefit? And, perhaps, what will they "lose" or lose out on if they choose not to adopt my claim?

I: Assigning a Persuasive Essay

Different Types of Appeals

Have students move into groups of three and choose one of the following scenarios to work with. As a group they should decide on their claim. Then, working either individually or as a group, they should develop reasons, using each of the three kinds of audience appeals. Each student should write a paragraph or two developing one reason, deliberately appealing to the audience emotionally, ethically, or logically.

Possible scenarios:

- Persuade your parents to let you go to a concert with friends on a school night.

- Persuade your parents to let you have the family car. You recently put a dent in the front fender or got a speeding ticket for going fifteen miles an hour over the limit.

- Persuade your sister to loan you twenty-five dollars.

- Persuade your teacher to accept your homework late.

- Persuade your boss to give you a raise.

Have groups combine to share their claims and reasons, and to see whether they recognize the kind of appeal each writer is using.

"Who Cares?" Understanding Your Audience

Students will need a selection of newspaper and magazine advertisements for this section. These may be brought into class by students, but can also be supplied by the teacher.

1. To introduce the strategies writers use to develop their reasons, select a few advertisements and ask the following:

   - "What specific audience is being targeted—gender, age, income level? How do you know?"

   - "What assumptions have the advertisement writers made about their targeted audience?"

     For instance, an ad might show that the writers are assuming that teenagers are interested in wearing shoes that sports heroes wear, that parents are interested in choosing more nutritious fast food for their children, or that fans who watch football also drink beer.

   - "How are the writers trying to appeal to the audience—emotionally, ethically, logically?"

   At this point students should be able to recognize these appeals in the advertisements. Remind them of the work they did in working with the previous scenarios, and reiterate that the type of appeal a writer chooses will depend on the topic, the situation, and the audience. Some audiences will place a higher value on logical appeals, but ethical and emotional appeals are equally effective when they are used fairly by writers. In most instances writers try to use a mix of the three.

2. Have students list some of the specific strategies writers use to develop their appeals and support their positions (e.g., anecdotes, scenarios, examples, etc.). Students should understand that writers use these strategies alone and in combination to

make emotional, ethical, and/or logical appeals that will convince audiences to seriously consider their claims.

3. Have students move into pairs or small groups to analyze advertisements using the following chart. Each group should analyze at least three ads. They should work together making notes as they look closely at the strategies used in the ads.

Analysis of an Advertisement				
Product Advertised:				
Assumptions about Audience		**How I Know**		
Reason to buy	**How reason is shown** (words, images, pictures, etc.)	**Kind of appeal** (emotional, ethical, logical)	**Strategy used**	**Effectiveness** (rate 1–5)

4. Have groups present the analysis of one advertisement to the class, or have groups combine to discuss and share their analyses.

5. Have students review their analyses of the advertisements, now specifically identifying the various strategies used to persuade in each advertisement.

Matching Strategies to Audience

Now students will choose a product from one of the ads they have analyzed and rewrite the text to target a new audience. For example, they might try to sell athletic shoes to senior citizens, or cleaning products to children.

Tell them to begin by selecting a new target audience for their product. They might ask themselves such questions as:

- What assumptions can I make about that audience?
- What kind of appeal will be most effective with this audience?

■ What strategies might work most effectively in creating that
   appeal?

Next students rewrite the text of the advertisement to appeal to a new
audience. They must be sure that their claim is clear, and use a combination of strategies to develop their appeal to their selected audience.

Follow-Up

Working with partners, have students identify the elements of persuasion in their classmate's rewritten ad:

■ Issue (in this case, the product)

■ Targeted audience

■ Assumptions being made about that audience

■ Claim

■ Kind of appeal

■ Strategies used to develop that appeal

Have students revise their advertisements as needed.

II: Writing a Persuasive Argument

Choosing Sides: Discovering What You Think

Open by reiterating that before they can determine what they *think* about
a subject, students must first clarify how they *feel* about it. They must,
in other words, discover their personal opinions on a subject before they
can discover arguable claims—their positions—on the issue.

Explain that they will make a chart designed to help them do three
things:

1. Discover a subject or issue that interests them. Tell them that
   sometimes the subject will be assigned or will arise as part of a
   project; other times (as in today's lesson) it might arise from a
   situation they experienced, read about, or heard about.

2. Discover how they feel about that subject—their personal opinion about it.

3. Transform that personal opinion into an arguable claim.

Give students time in class to complete the chart, entering at least three
possible subjects. They may use this form or some equivalent chart form:

Subjects of Interest	Feelings about the Subjects (Personal Opinions)	Arguable Claims

When students have completed their charts, have them share their subjects and issues with partners or in small groups. Generate a list of issues and subjects on the board that students may want to use as subjects for persuasive papers. They should consider the following questions as they advise one another on focusing and defining their issues:

- Is the issue clear and arguable? Is it stated as a question? For example:

    Subject: Drug testing

    Possible Issue: "Should student athletes be subjected to mandatory random drug testing?"

    Possible Issue: "Should all school personnel, students, teachers, administrators, etc., be subjected to random mandatory drug testing?"

    Possible Issue: "Why isn't mandatory drug testing an invasion of privacy?"

- Is the claim clear and forcefully stated?

    Ineffective claim (opinion of personal preference; not arguable): "I don't like the idea of drug testing."

    Ineffective claim: (fails to take a position; not arguable): "There are both pros and cons to drug testing."

    Effective Claim: Schools have no right to subject athletes to mandatory random drug testing.

    Effective Claim: To subject athletes to mandatory random drug testing is not only prejudicial, it will do little to prevent drug use. (This claim not only summarizes a position, it points to main supporting reasons for the position.)

"What's Wrong with This Picture?" Recognizing Flawed Reasoning

When students are confident that their claims are arguable, ask, "Once you've identified the specific issue, and have clarified your position on it, how do you develop the argument and defend your claim so others will take you seriously?" Explain that *reasons* are the main points supporting the claim—the *because* of the position the writer is taking. These reasons need *evidence* in order to be convincing.

Emphasize that the most important parts of a persuasive paper are the reasons and the evidence, and tell students they may have to research their issues in order to find evidence to support their claims. Simply having an arguable claim doesn't mean that it is well-supported or even valid; to be convincing the claim needs to be backed by evidence that goes beyond the writer's personal experiences, beliefs, and preferences, and this means the writer must be extremely well-informed about the issue. Without rational, informed reasons, and relevant evidence to back them up, even the best persuasive techniques will amount only to fancy packages without substance.

Working with newspapers, magazines, junk mail, etc., whether provided by you or your students, students should work in pairs to find examples of at least five fallacies in an advertisement or other written document. They should complete the chart below, citing each example of faulty reasoning, identifying the fallacy and explaining how the reasoning is flawed, and telling how they would reply to show that the statement is not logical.

Quote the statement or describe the visual.	Where did you find it?	Identify the fallacy and explain why the reasoning is faulty.	How would you reply?

As students share their examples and discuss the kinds of fallacies represented, they will probably see that there are not always clear distinctions between what is reasonable and persuasive and what is faulty and manipulative. Point out that there are many issues about which reasonable people will disagree, and there is seldom absolute proof that one way of thinking is better than another. A writer's goal is to present the opinion rationally and fairly so that readers understand and seriously consider it, even if in the end they don't agree.

Collecting Evidence

Open by asking students to consider what kinds of things make convincing evidence. Ask, "Where does evidence come from?"

- From personal experience
- From reading or observation (television, movies, etc.)
- From things you've learned in class—from lectures
- From others' experiences
- From secondary sources
- From experts you have read or talked to

Remind students of the main kinds of evidence they worked with earlier (facts, statistics, examples, expert opinion) and emphasize that the most effective persuasive papers use a mix of these.

Emphasize the following points about evidence:

- It must be specific. Statements about what "everyone" does or what "always" happens are easy to disprove.
- It must be objective. Just as with claims, evidence arising from personal preference or belief is not arguable. Just the fact that you believe it does not make it so.
- It must be relevant to and supportive of the claim.

Tell students not to be afraid of revising their claims or even their issues if they have trouble finding effective reasons or evidence. If they cannot come up with evidence, they will not be able to persuade others to take their positions seriously.

Point–Counterpoint: "Listening" to the Opposition

In this lesson students work with a partner to anticipate and address possible counterarguments to their claims.

Have students share their claims, reasons, and evidence with a partner. Then they should play "Devil's Advocate" for each other in order to discover and address possible counterarguments to their claims, and to complete their point–counterpoint charts. Point out that they might find they have to revise their reasons and/or their evidence as they explore the other side of their argument.

Be sure students understand that they do not need a counterargument for each piece of evidence they include, or even for every reason; but they should be able to argue against themselves effectively, so they can show their audience that they understand and have seriously considered all angles of the argument before deciding on their positions. For example:

Claim: Congress should not pass a law making tobacco an illegal substance.			
Reason	**Evidence**	**Counterargument**	**Answer to Counterargument**
The law is unenforceable	Fact: It is already against the law for people under eighteen to buy tobacco products, but teens still have no trouble accessing these.	At least the law makes a strong public statement, and it does affect *some* people	There are more effective ways of making this statement, for example, education.

When students have completed their charts, they should rank the reasons from the most effective to the least effective. This ranking will come in handy later when they decide how to order their papers.

Assignment:

- State your claim about the issue.
- Write a paragraph or two explaining one reason for your claim.
- Offer evidence in support of your reason, and be sure to acknowledge and address possible counterarguments.

Organizing and Drafting the Essay

Now that students have gathered the ideas and information they need to support their positions, it is time to organize that information. Emphasize that there are many different ways of structuring a persuasive essay. The way a writer chooses will depend on his or her subject matter and the specific purpose and situation that give rise to the essay.

Remind students that their persuasive essays should have the following components:

1. An introduction, a body, and a conclusion.

2. An objective explanation of the issue, especially complex issues, so that readers can clearly understand the situation.

3. A claim that clearly states the writer's position or opinion on the issue.

4. A series of rational secondary claims, clearly stating reasons for the writer's major claim.

5. Specific evidence—facts and examples—that directly develops and explains each of the reasons. The evidence should be of different types and should be drawn from a variety of sources.

6. Explicit acknowledgment of opposing viewpoints, with answers to possible counterarguments to the writer's claim.

7. A solid and concise conclusion that summarizes the writer's position.

These components will be evident in any rubric to assess the persuasive essay, as in the one on pages 57–59. Teachers may wish to design a rubric with their students or give them one created by their department or school district. Since students have seen this list evolve during their study, they will be able to participate in self-assessment as well as understanding the teacher's critique. To involve students in such self-assessment, have them fill out the self-assessment chart in the appendix on page 60 and follow up with the self-assessment essay.

Sample Student Persuasive Essay

The following essay by Brittany Waxman, grade 10, was written as preparation for a speech.

> To Brush or Not to Brush
>
> Do you want to have teeth with bright red inflamed gums? Do you want teeth that are rotting away in your mouth? Do you want to feel all of the pain of having those problems? You probably don't want to deal with any of that. Most likely you would rather have teeth like a model, perfectly white and straight. That is why you should brush your teeth.
>
> There are many reasons for brushing your teeth with toothpaste. One big reason is just because clean teeth look better. According to Rebecca Spencer a dental hygienist, "Brushing twice a day for two minutes helps prevent tooth decay and periodontal disease." Brushing also removes plaque. Plaque is a sticky film of bacteria that accumulates on your teeth and releases acids that eat away at them. A build up of plaque can cause cavities and if it

is left on too long, it may turn into calculus or tartar. Calculus is a hard and chunky substance that is bad for your teeth. It may cause your gums to become swollen or bloody and makes it harder to floss. Brushing helps prevent tooth decay which is what causes cavities and many tooth aches. Brushing with toothpaste promotes remineralization. Remineralization is replacing the minerals in your teeth and it can only be done by using toothpaste because tooth enamel has no contact with the bloodstream. Brushing also cleans and polishes your teeth and removes stains. It even freshens your breath. Brushing helps avoid the dentist. According to Rebecca Spencer, "Brushing combined with flossing helps you to avoid uncomfortable and painful dental procedures."

It is important that when you brush, you brush properly. The correct way to brush has several steps. The first step is to put a pea-sized amount of toothpaste on the brush. Using only that much is recommended by dentists because too much toothpaste causes fluorosis which causes white splotches on your teeth. You should also rinse and spit. The second step is to place the toothbrush against your gum line (where the teeth and gums meet) at a 45-degree angle. Then use small circular motions to brush your teeth and gums. After that you should brush the inner surfaces or backs of your front teeth with the front part of your toothbrush. Brush back and forth on the chewing surfaces of your teeth holding the brush flat. You should always brush gently. Rebecca Spencer the dental hygienist says that, "Brushing with too hard of a toothbrush or too vigorously can cause receding gums which can lead to tooth sensitivity and root decay not to mention unsightly smiles." Just like the waves erode a beach, hard brushing erodes your gums. Gums do not come back unless you have them surgically grafted. Grafting is taking gum tissue from one part of your mouth and adding it to where your gums have receded.

You should also use the right kind of toothbrush. It should have soft, nylon, round ended bristles. The bristles shouldn't scratch or irritate your gums. Toothbrushes can wear out and you should replace them often. It is recommended for people to replace them every three to four months or when the bristles become worn or frayed. Children and people with braces usually wear them out sooner.

Remember your choices. One choice is having ugly and painful teeth and needing to go to the dentist all the time. Your other choice is having beautiful and pain-free teeth. There is only one question that you have to ask yourself. To brush or not to brush, that is the question.

Persuasive Essay: A Sample Middle and High School Rubric, 5-point scale:

Criteria	Score Point 5 Exceeds Expectations	Score Point 4 Meets Expectations
Position	Score point 5 meets all the criteria listed in score point 4. In addition, a paper receiving this score presents unusually perceptive arguments and richly elaborated supports.	Position: ■ asserts and maintains clear position through-out the piece ■ presents evidence and explanations in a purposeful way
Organization and Coherence	Such papers show the use of lively and precise language selected with careful attention to persuasive appeal. They show confidence, conviction, and enthusiasm. A score point 5 paper argues effectively for its position and shows an unusually insightful sense of possible reader concerns. These exceptional papers show a flair for persuasion resulting from interesting ideas expressed in an original way.	Organization and Coherence: ■ establishes a plausible context for the presenta-tion of their ideas. ■ arranges details, reasons, examples, and/or anecdotes effectively and persuasively ■ may present ideas in unusual or surprising patterns ■ possesses overall coherence and internal cohesion
Elaboration ■ **Depth/Density of Argument** ■ **Relevance of Argument** ■ **Audience Awareness**		Elaboration: ■ thoroughly develops and elaborates one or more reasons ■ uses a variety of strategies such as examples, anecdotes, and other kinds of information ■ supports argument(s) with richly detailed reasons selected to support the arguments forcefully ■ embeds prior knowl-edge, personal experi-ence, and/or reflection into fabric of argument ■ presents arguments with a clear awareness of reader concerns ■ shows credibility and authority by stating sources of information ■ anticipates and addresses possible reader misconceptions or counterarguments

continued on next page

Persuasive Essay Rubric continued

Criteria	Score Point 3 Needs Revision	Score Point 2 Needs Instruction
Position	Position: ■ states a clear position ■ presents some purposeful evidence and explanations ■ may have digressions	Position: ■ may be irresolute in identifying a position ■ may meander and contain digressions
Organization and Coherence	Organization and Coherence: ■ establishes a context ■ arranges ideas in simple ways, often relying on lists ■ organization may seem imposed rather than organic ■ possesses overall coherence but cohesion between sentences or paragraphs may suffer from lack of transitions	Organization and Coherence: ■ may show some discernible pattern or plan ■ arguments or ideas may appear to be organized because of use of external organizational markers ("In the first place," etc.) ■ may have related arguments in a haphazard way ■ may lack overall coherence by omitting a clear beginning or ending
Elaboration ■ **Depth/Density of Argument** ■ **Relevance of Argument** ■ **Audience Awareness**	Elaboration: ■ states appropriate reasons ■ uses some variety of strategies such as examples, anecdotes, personal testimony to support arguments ■ may use supporting reasons that are not clearly relevant ■ assumes that readers will find the ideas credible ■ uses appropriate language but may lack precision ■ usually conveys a sense of conviction but may not give sources of information ■ may be scant or superficial evidence of reader awareness	Elaboration: ■ presents some information but may lack elaboration ■ may contain irrelevant and/or inappropriate details, examples, and/or arguments ■ usually does not reflect an awareness of the reader ■ language is generally predictable and general rather than precise

Criteria	Score Point 1 Needs a Lot of Instruction	Score Point 0 Unscorable
Position	Position: ■ may be so brief that direction is difficult to discern ■ may take a position but it is not elaborated ■ may be long, rambling, and unfocused	Paper is unscorable as it shows only a vague (if any) discernible position. No arguments are presented. There is no evidence of reader awareness. Paper may address reader on matter relating to the writing prompt or express ideas about the process of having to write at all.
Organization and Coherence	Organization and Coherence: ■ usually shows little logical arrangement of ideas ■ may be too brief to discern pattern of organization ■ may possess simple, straightforward organization	
Elaboration ■ **Depth/Density of Argument** ■ **Relevance of Argument** ■ **Audience Awareness**	Elaboration: ■ argument is thinly developed ■ uses few supportive ideas ■ contains few relevant arguments ■ often assumes that the reader already knows what the writer thinks ■ usually contains clichés and predictable vocabulary; language may be inappropriate or inexact	

Note

1. Newspapers and magazines are the most obvious sources for persuasive essays. Most English textbooks also have a number of persuasive essays that can be used in the assignments in this chapter.

Appendix: End-of-Term Student Self-Assessment Chart

Fill out the chart by naming or describing papers or projects completed this term. For each item, use the numbers 1 (low) to 5 (high) to indicate the four aspects of your involvement. Following completion of the chart, write the Self-Assessment Essay.

Paper or Project: Title or Brief Description	Level of Interest	Level of Value	Degree of Participation	Quality of Participation

Student Self-Assessment Essay

After students have filled out this chart, they write a self-evaluation essay reflecting on their work for the past term and articulating ideas about what they hope to achieve in the next. They refer specifically to papers and projects listed in the chart, elaborating on their assessments of a paper/project's interest or value; commenting on reasons for their lack of involvement, perhaps; explaining why they have assessed the quality of their work as they have.

As a conclusion to the self-assessment essay, students look at the totality of their involvement and work over the term and, in schools where letter grades are part of the reporting system, assign a letter grade to their work for the term. They know that any disparity with the teacher's evaluation, after the teacher has reviewed their charts and read their essays, will lead to a conference. Ideally, the teacher would confer with each student about his or her grade; realistically, given the student load in many high schools, it may not be possible to confer with each student at the end of each grading period. This compromise assumes, of course, that there will have been teacher/student conferences periodically throughout the term.

Suggested Directions to Students

After you have filled out this chart, write a self-evaluation essay reflecting on your work for the past term and articulating ideas about what you hope to achieve in the next. Refer specifically to papers and projects listed in the chart, elaborating on your assessments of a paper/project's interest or value; commenting on reasons for your lack of involvement, perhaps; explaining why you have assessed the quality of your work as you have.

As a conclusion to the self-assessment essay, look at the totality of your involvement and work over the term and assign a letter grade to your work for the term. You know that we will discuss your grade if I have come to a different evaluation of your work for this term.

Self-assessment chart and essay assignment are reprinted from *A Measure of Success: From Assignment to Assessment in English Language Arts* by Fran Claggett (Portsmouth, NH: Heinemann, 1996).

5 Evaluation

Joan Brown

In evaluation the writer presents a judgment based on a critical assessment of a subject. The judgment is supported by a convincing, well-reasoned discussion, using specific criteria. In an effective evaluation the writer speaks with authority on the subject. While evaluation may be thought of as a subcategory of persuasion, it is often taught as a genre in itself. Some evaluation activities and strategies are included in the persuasive practices, but this section isolates it and treats it as a separate genre.

Students are constantly making decisions—about clothes, about activities, about relationships. When they become adults, students will be faced with making decisions about whether to go to college and, if so, what college to apply to. They will be making decisions about jobs and careers, marriage, children—all aspects of day-to-day living. Exploring decisions in writing can help them focus on using sound evaluative procedures before they make final decisions. The processes to be learned through writing effective evaluations have both current and life-long implications.

Features of Evaluation

Judgment

A judgment is based on the thoughtful examination of the subject. Implied or stated, the judgment makes an assertion about the subject's worth.

Evaluation is more than the simple expression of likes or dislikes. Although personal preference may be a factor, evaluation depends on a critical assessment of the subject based on logically formulated criteria.

Criteria

The selection of criteria, which focus on the subject's importance or unique qualities, is crucial. The writer may choose criteria that are associated with the subject: for example, in evaluating vacation destinations, the writer would traditionally examine climate, points of interest, and cost. In a testing situation, students may be asked to evaluate the quality or appropriateness of a poem or short story using criteria previously determined by the teacher, the class, or an external authority. Often, however, the writer must develop his or her own criteria.

The category of the subject often helps determine criteria. For instance, in deciding which of two movies is more successful, the writer may select "socially significant" or "technically innovative" as the dominant criterion. The writer of a successful evaluation presents criteria clearly and applies them consistently.

Evidence

An evaluation must present clearly stated, well-developed, and well-supported evidence. Some useful strategies:

- compare and contrast subjects in the same category
- include personal experience or the experience of others
- cite authorities
- cite lines from a text
- observe specimens, as in a study of plants and animals
- note procedures in experiments

Audience

Awareness of audience, which determines how much and what type of background information the writer must include, governs the strategies that writers should use. The writer should maintain a consistently authoritative tone. Although writers may introduce other points of view as they build their arguments, they always keep their own positions clear. To orient and accommodate the reader to the subject being evaluated, the writer may use a variety of strategies such as the following:

- devise beginnings that clearly acquaint readers with the subject
- describe the subject, its characteristics and significance
- provide information the audience may not know
- describe personal experiences or feelings associated with them
- address the audience's concerns
- direct some concluding remarks to the audience

Teaching Activities for Evaluation

1. Generating Criteria, Reasons, and Evidence

Students need practice in generating criteria, in stating a claim of judgment, and in building arguments. They need to understand the concept of *criteria:* standards for judging something. Criteria apply to a class of things, not to individuals in the class. If students are to evaluate a fast-food restaurant, their criteria must be appropriate for fast-food restaurants, not for gourmet restaurants. Criteria must be impersonal, not based merely on personal tastes, and they must be appropriate to the thing being evaluated.

Suggestions for One Sequence of Activities

Introduce the students to the subject of evaluation. Ask each person to write down the name of the best movie he or she has ever seen. Then have them cluster the reasons why it was a good movie. Tell them that these are the criteria by which they have judged the movie.

Have a topic on the board when you begin this lesson. In five minutes, have students list criteria, generating as many as they can.

Topics might include:

What makes a good pizza?

What qualities make a good TV program?

What makes a book worth reading?

What are the qualities of a good friend?

What qualities would you look for in a new car?

What qualities make a group popular?

2. Conducting the Workshop

Have each group select a subject and generate criteria by which they could judge this subject. For example, criteria for an effective movie might include

- story line
- theme
- unity and consistency
- technical innovation
- acting
- character development
- cinematography

- direction
- relevance to audience

Students might select a subgenre; for example, horror movies or space movies rather than movies in general.

In summation, review the elements that make evaluations effective. You might call this discussion "Beyond 'I like it' or 'I hate it' conversations."

Planning the Evaluation

To open the discussion, have each student select a subject for evaluation: it might be a book, a movie, a restaurant, a sports team, a sports star, a brand of shoes, a music group, etc. Here they select a specific subject rather than a general category.

For the workshop, students should first *make a claim or judgment* about their subject. (They might select two subjects to compare.) Then they must consider the criteria they will use to make their evaluations. After they explain their criteria with reasons for that judgment, they list the factual evidence they can offer to support these reasons. Give them a model of a chart to use in planning their evaluations:

Topic:		
Judgment:		
Criteria	**Reasons**	**Evidence**

If they are writing a comparison, they would say that Brand X is better than Brand Y, then go on to establish criteria, reasons, and evidence. In this case, they might use this kind of chart:

Topic:			
Judgment Statement: (Brand X is superior to Brand Y)			
	Criteria	**Reasons**	**Evidence**
Brand X			
Brand Y			

Drafting the Essay

Have students draft an article for an appropriate publication, possibly a magazine, evaluating their topic. The article should convince readers of the advantages or benefits of the product or service by establishing convincing criteria and providing evidence for their judgment.

Reviewing the First Draft

Once students have finished their drafts, they should look at the following questions:

- Audience's knowledge of the subject:
  - How much knowledge of the subject do I expect the reader to have?
  - What kinds of information will I need to supply so that the reader will accept my evaluation?
- Criteria:
  - Are my criteria appropriate to the subject I am evaluating?
  - What further evidence do I need to strengthen my evaluation?
- Organization:
  - How might I capture my reader's attention?
  - How can I sequence my reasons so that they effectively support my judgment?

◆ What is irrelevant or ineffective in my paper that I could cut?

◆ How should I end my paper—by summarizing my reasons, by restating my judgment, or by using some other strategy?

In summation: Have students write a short statement of how they can improve their papers.

3: Response Groups

Be sure students understand their roles in this process. The purpose of responding is to assist the writer, to provide a frame for the writer to rethink his or her essay. The writer always has the right to maintain ownership of the paper, selecting and discarding advice as he or she sees fit.

This revision guide may serve to remind the writer of points covered in the discussion about evaluation. Have response partners answer these questions in conversation with the writer or have response partners write answers to these questions as a basis for discussion.

Response Group Guidelines

- State the subject of evaluation.
- State the writer's judgment of this subject.
- List the criteria used for the evaluation.
- Comment on the criteria.
    ◆ Are they appropriate?
    ◆ Do they cover the major aspects of the subject?
    ◆ Are they relevant?
- Look at the writer's support for his or her judgment. Make a general statement about the effectiveness of the support. Is it logical? Does it flow from one point to the next or does it seem choppy or disorganized? Do you need more information to be convinced of the judgment?
- Comment on the opening of the paper. Does it capture your interest?
- What might make this a more interesting, more effective evaluation?

Students take responsibility for writing their final evaluations using whatever seems relevant from the response-group critique.

In summation: Assessment of evaluation essays is based on the criteria established at the beginning of this section: orienting readers, judgment, criteria, and evidence.

Extension Assignments

Extension 1: Students are often asked to write evaluation essays in response to literature. This might be a good time to review how what they have learned about writing this kind of essay will transfer to writing about a book or a character. Here are two sample assignments that we might give our students in an English class:

Assignment 1 (Students have read at least ten poems of their own choice.):

Select a poem from those you have read. Think about what qualities make a good poem. Then decide whether you think this poem should be included in a book to be entitled, "Best Poems for Young Adults." (Notice that you were not asked whether you like this poem!)

Write an essay evaluating this poem. Give reasons for your judgment and support your reasons with details from the poem itself. Be sure to use several exact quotations from the poem. Convince your teacher that your judgment is a thoughtful one.

Assignment 2 (Students have read two novels with similar themes.):

Decide which of the two novels you think deals more effectively with the theme of (state theme). Give reasons for your judgment and use citations from the novels to support your ideas. Convince students in your class that if they had to read only one of these novels, it should be (title).

Extension 2: A Book, Movie, or Restaurant Review

Analyzing Published Reviews

Assemble a selection of restaurant, movie, and book reviews from a variety of publications. Try to have a sampling from publications that are written for different audiences. It is best if the students bring in the reviews, but reviews can also be supplied by the teacher.

Tell students that a review is one kind of evaluation essay in which the reviewer is helping the readers decide how to spend their time and money. Evaluators must establish criteria on which they will base their judgments, present their judgments, and justify their opinions with reasons and evidence to show how the subjects meet or fail to meet the stated criteria.

Though reviewers may not urge readers to a take a particular action, they do offer clear judgments about a subject; and they try to influence readers to consider those judgments when deciding on a course of action. So, though differing somewhat in the details, reviews are as much a type of persuasion as are argumentative essays; therefore, people who write reviews must include the same components and follow the same processes as those who write other kinds of persuasion. Help students see how to apply the principles of persuasion to this evaluation assignment.

- The subject, in this case the specific book, movie, or restaurant you will review.

- The audience—whom are you trying to influence?

- The claim is your considered judgment of the subject.

   Evaluation is more than the simple expression of likes and dislikes. (Remember: personal preferences are not arguable— and to write persuasion you need an *arguable* claim.) Although personal preference may be a factor, evaluation depends on a critical assessment of the subject based on criteria or standards that are logically formulated and relevant to the subject.

- Criteria on which to measure the subject being evaluated.

   Criteria are standards for judging something. They apply to a class of things, not to individuals in the class. If, for example, you are going to review a horror film, your criteria must be appropriate for horror films, not for romantic comedies. For your evaluation to be persuasive—to influence readers—it must seem informed and convincing; and to be convincing it must be based on appropriate criteria.

- The reasons are statements of how and/or why the subject meets or fails to meet your stated criteria.

- The evidence might include facts, examples, illustrations, anecdotes, details, and/or comparisons to similar products or situations, to explain and validate your claim about why the subject does or does not meet your criteria.

- The counterarguments might raise questions about the appropriateness of your criteria and/or about your assessment of the subject.

Give students time in class to read and analyze some published reviews, looking specifically at how writers present and manipulate these components. They should read at least one movie review, one book review, and one restaurant review. Then, working with a partner, they should make notes to identify each of the required elements of an evaluation essay. Tell them that, in a sense, they are evaluating the review as they complete this exercise.

A Student's Evaluation

Here is an essay written outside of class about a much-loved book, *Night* by Elie Wiesel (New York: Hill, 1960). Bryan, grade 6, loves this book so much that he carries it around in his backpack and has read it "about a hundred times." When I suggested that I would like to read what he had to say about it, he sat down and produced this evaluative essay with no instruction.

My Opinion about the Autobiography, *Night*

by Bryan Waxman

Night was, shall I say, terrible yet at the same time perfect in a way I can't explain. Since there were many things that I could relate to, to help me understand. Though there were quite a few words I couldn't understand, I could ask my parents, that's what they're there for. To really contemplate, and grasp the book, I found quite hard at first, but after that it sucks you in keeping you up all night with its terror. Even after you finish the book you can't fall asleep, because you're thinking of all the horror Adolph Hitler put the Jewish people through. If you end up falling asleep you have nightmares about it, so anyway you think of it, you're going to end up being startled by it.

The book *Night* really put into perspective how life for the Jews was back in the early forties. The main character lost all of his kin making life tough even after their liberation.

Night was a horrifying book in things like how they would torture and kill the Jewish people. They would even burn people alive in the Nazi's open fire crematories, they also did many other horrible, fatal things that were more universal back then, like hanging. Don't go off thinking they were nice to the Jews before they killed them though, because they practically starved them with lack of food. When the main character, Elie, worked in the kitchen with his friend, they would sneak potato peelings so as not to starve or to get too weak to work. If they got too weak to work the Nazis would kill them. The other tragic thing was that the potato peelings would go in to the Jew's soup, and the actual potatoes would go into the Nazi's soup. Why did the very undeserving people end up with the better things? Unfortunately that's how the world still is today; hopefully someday in the future there will be more justice.

When the Jews first entered the camp they had to get their heads shaved, and do you know how the mattresses were made? That's right, with human hair from everywhere on the body! So with the mattresses made from human hair, as you could imagine, they were uncomfortable, and itchy.

When the Nazis were under attack, of course they fled, making the Jews run hundreds of miles, and shooting anyone tired or going too slow. Eventually they were caught, beginning liberation.

Though Elie was a strong man he did get hurt once, and had to go to the medical center with his injured leg, while he was there the place just got fuller and fuller, forcing the Nazis to inject them with poison to kill them. With Elie's consciousness, and quick wittedness, he hastily realized the injection made the men have a heart attack, then expire, so he quickly said he felt better, and then struggled out the door.

This is a great book if you're interested in things like huge incidents. This book is also good for people who want history reality.

Self-Assessment: Another Evaluative Essay

For this section, you may want to refer to the self-assessment chart and assignment in the appendix to Chapter 4. Alternatively, you can prepare your own chart for student self-assessment.

After students have completed the chart, have them write a self-evaluation essay reflecting on their work throughout the study. They should refer to specific assignments and papers they have completed, elaborating on their assessments of a paper or activity's value or lack of value to them and explaining why they have assessed the quality of their work as they have.

As a conclusion to the self-assessment essay, you might have students look at the totality of their involvement and work throughout the study of evaluation and assign a letter grade to their work for this study.

6 Reflection

Writing reflective essays requires the ability to see connections. Moving from a personal experience or a general concept, the writer explores possibilities, tries out ideas, and reaches beyond personal implications to an idea with a larger, more general significance. In reflection, writers push at the limits of thought, disregarding glib understandings, trite expressions of hope, or easy moralistic answers. They explore what it is that we have in common beyond the superficial, looking for some insights toward larger truths.

The reflective essay often begins incognito: It may begin as autobiography, then use a personal experience to reflect about life in general. It may begin as speculation about a particular situation, then use these speculations to explore the implications of the "whys" and the "what-ifs." Reflection may begin in interpretation as a search for meaning, then use these meanings to reach broader understandings. It may begin as evaluation, proclaiming a judgment, then explore the ramifications of the judgment. This kind of writing is a shape-shifter, hard to pin down, but easy to recognize in its eventual form.

Features of a Reflective Essay

The reflective essay has two parts, often interwoven—the occasion for reflection and the reflection itself.

The Occasion for Reflection: A Thing Seen, Read, or Experienced

Occasions for reflection might be observations of a natural phenomenon, an experience with another person or group of persons, a quotation, or perhaps a familiar proverb. The occasion becomes the stimulus for the writer to explore and interpret some aspect of people in general or of the natural world.

Strategies for presenting the occasion might include

- description using concrete language and sensory detail;
- narrative strategies such as pacing, dialogue, and action;
- a citation giving the location of original quotation or subject; and

- a web of related, parallel commentaries.

It is important to note that the reflective essay does not follow a formulaic pattern in organization. While there are some patterns that may recur in reflective essays, the pattern arises from the way the writer thinks about the subject, and evolves as the essay progresses. On rethinking, the writer may observe a pattern that she or he wishes to emphasize and rework the paper to that effect, but the pattern emerges, it is not imposed. The organizing structure must be appropriate to the writer's purpose and audience. The reflections must not seem to be simply statements that exemplify an initial thesis or preestablished position, as might be true in a persuasive, interpretive, or evaluative essay.

Possibilities for reflection might include

- extended exploration of the subject;
- explicit, insightful generalizations; or
- implicit, embedded generalization based on extended narration.

Some Patterns Reflective Essays May Take

Teachers who analyzed many student reflective essays in designing study guides and rubrics for the California Assessment Program found that four patterns were characteristic of large groups of the papers. These patterns were not imposed, but discovered by the teachers who studied the papers. Here are the patterns they found: The writer may

- present the occasion (narrate a full incident or describe an observation), choosing details and images carefully as a way to ground the reflection that follows. The reflection then moves off on its own, perhaps with some reference to the initiating occasion.
- launch an occasion but then move in and out of it along the way, reflecting on the ideas it suggests.
- construct a web of related, often parallel experiences or observations that show, by their interrelatedness, a theme underlying common human experiences
- begin with a quotation, proverb, or general statement and explore its ideas with a series of personal observations or experiences, reflecting on how each connects to the general concept.

Teaching Activities for the Reflective Essay

I: Concrete and Abstract: Understanding the Concepts

Reflective essays are grounded in the concrete but explore abstractions. It is a good idea for teachers to spend a little time clarifying the concepts of *concrete* and *abstract* through activities before getting into reading and writing reflective essays.

Concrete/Abstract Activity

Open this activity by reading aloud a simple, imagistic poem such as "The Red Wheelbarrow," by William Carlos Williams. Then ask students to make notes about the poem while reading it to themselves.

- Have the students draw or sketch the picture that this poem presents. Emphasize that they should put everything they can *see* into their drawings. These elements are the *concrete images*.
- Now ask them to list all of the concrete words.
- What words are left over? Ask them to talk about the meaning of these words. How are these words related to the concrete images?
- Finally, ask them what it could be that is represented by the words "so much." There is, of course, no possible "right" answer here, but students should be able to come up with a list of *abstractions* that might be represented by "so much." (If using a poem other than "The Red Wheelbarrow," substitute whatever fits.)
- Now, ask students to try reading the poem again with the *abstract* word they like best as the title of the poem.
- As a final step in this exercise, ask students to write a page *reflecting* on the meaning of the poem. They should use their selected *abstract word* as the subject of their reflections and the *concrete images* to help elaborate their ideas.

Making an Abstraction Concrete

Now, reverse the procedure of the last exercise and begin with the abstract word. Ask students to identify an abstraction that is important in their lives. They will probably come up with words like *love, friendship, privacy, time, independence, freedom, prejudice*.

- Next, have students draw their abstractions. They may be uncertain at first, depending on whether they have had experience in doing graphics, but most students will settle down quickly and sketch a concrete image that stands for their abstraction.

- Ask them to title their drawing with the name of their abstraction.

- The next step is extremely important: in small groups, have them talk about, *reflect* on, how their abstractions are portrayed by their drawings.

- In their journals, have them write a short reflection on this activity.

As an extension of this activity: Have students write a short poem portraying the concrete images in their drawings but include, if they can, a brief allusion to the abstraction, as Williams does with the words "so much depends." They should title their poems with the name of the abstraction, then share them with other students.

II: Reading and Modeling Reflective Essays

Students will read, analyze, and then use as models the elements that are important in generating a reflective essay.

Identifying Elements: Concrete, Abstract, Reflective

Have students read a short essay that is accessible in both content and language. Essays about the natural world are especially appropriate for reflection. As an example, use the short essay "Winter," by Henry David Thoreau. Students should have copies of whatever essay you are using.

Read the essay aloud, asking students to make notes as they listen, identifying the elements of reflection.

"Winter," by Henry David Thoreau

I wish to hear the silence of the night, for the silence is something positive and to be heard. I cannot walk with my ears covered. I must stand still and listen with open ears, far from the noises of the village, that the night may make its impression on me. A fertile and eloquent silence. Sometimes the silence is merely negative, an arid and barren waste in which I shudder, where no ambrosia grows. I must hear the whispering of a myriad voices. Silence alone is worthy to be heard. Silence is of various depths and fertility, like soil. Now it is a mere Sahara, where men perish of hunger and thirst, now a fertile bottom, or prairie, of the West. As I leave the village, drawing nearer to the woods, I listen from time to time to hear the hounds of Silence baying the moon,—to know if they are on the track of any game. If there's no Diana in the night, what is it worth? [. . .] The silence rings; it is musical and thrills me. A night in which the silence was audible, I heard the unspeakable. (Journal of 21 January 1853)

Now ask students to fill out a chart like this one:

Concrete Words	Abstractions	Reflections

Modeling an Essay on Thoreau's

Ask students to select a season to reflect on. They should think about an overarching abstraction, like Thoreau's *silence,* and write a short essay exploring their ideas. They should remember to use concrete images to ground their ideas.

Identifying Elements of Reflection in Student Essays

Working with partners, have students identify the elements of reflection in their essays: concrete images, abstractions, reflection. You might want them to make a chart for their own essays like the one they did for Thoreau's "Winter."

Correlative Activity: Reading and Writing Reflective Essays

Students who lack experience reading and writing the reflective essay usually fail to ground their reflections in concrete observations or personal anecdotes or do so only superficially and then write a conventional "expository" essay about the idea in the topic; they often narrate a relevant personal experience but then neglect to explore the idea it suggests or do so only briefly, often in a moralizing way. For these reasons it is useful to have students read extensively in connection with the study of writing reflective pieces.

Have students, working alone or in pairs, find and read from three to five reflective essays. They might look at magazines, newspapers, or collections of articles in the classroom library. Using the list of patterns presented above as guidelines, ask students to label the essays they read according to the patterns the authors have developed. In some cases, they may find that they have a pattern of development that does not fit into any of the four categories provided. In this case, they should name the new category and write a brief description of it.

They can make a chart such as this:

Title	Author	Subject of Essay	Pattern of Development	Interest Level (5 = high, 1 = low)

Building a Class List of Reflective Essays

Ask students to work in pairs to compare their charts. Expanding the groups to three or four, have them check each other for accuracy in determining the pattern of the essay.

As a class, look at the lists compiled. Do a brief summary of the kinds of development students found in the essays they read. Talk about any new patterns that they observed. Have all students add these new patterns to their lists.

You may want to collect the charts and put them together in a class folder that is accessible to all students. Students looking for essays to read could consult this list for essays with a high interest level.

Writing a Reflective Essay

Now that students are familiar with a number of possibilities for writing a reflective essay, give them the opportunity to write a more substantial essay of their own.

In writing a reflective essay, the student follows these steps:

- selecting a topic for a final reflective essay
- writing a draft of the essay

- analyzing their pattern of thought
- tightening the essay (deep editing)
- writing a final draft (revising)
- final editing (surface editing)
- sharing final draft with partner or small group

Have students okay their topics with you before beginning to write. You want to be sure that they have chosen topics they can really reflect on and not positions that they want to defend, as in the persuasive paper. Have them think about the kinds of *occasion* they might use as topics for their essays: *a thing seen, read, or experienced.*

When students have completed their first drafts, they should work with a partner in analyzing their patterns of thought and tightening the essay. This is the deep editing.

Students should check for coherence, style, and conventions (surface editing) before they put their essays into final form.

We suggest spending some time having students read one another's final papers. One strategy that makes this process helpful for the students is having each person who reads a paper write a short note on a self-stick note and put it on the paper. These notes should be signed. The final papers might be collected in a class book for more general reading.

Self-Assessment: Reflecting on Reflections

Have students fill out the self-assessment chart (see the appendix to Chapter 4 for a copy of the chart) and write the essay as described there.

"Mother Life, Mother Past": A Student's Reflections Create a Generational Portrait

Julia Ng wrote the following four pieces at various times during her junior year, in response to different readings and assignments from teacher Joan Brown. While revisiting her work to compile her end-of-the-year portfolio, she recognized them as parts of a single piece, and she included them in her portfolio under the above title. The projects included doing a mandala graphic assignment, which led to the first poem, and interviewing her mother, which led to the two reflective prose pieces.

Shadows

My eyes tightly shut,
as I try to understand
why she is what she is,
and
what she is like.

She stretches,
strains,
a bending, twisting tree.
Almost broken
but brimming with butterflies, orchids, life.
Wrapping themselves around her
ripened trunk,
they drink and drink
from the rich milk of her pithy
roots.
She is double happiness, double fortune,
double grief.
She is balanced flat on her feet,
but curves around
to gaze and gaze
at old footprints.

She is Spring,
fertile and luscious.
Even in the hard, chilled earth
she produces and nurtures,
furtively glancing about
as she tones down her bloom
from what was.

She is a waterfall,
engulfing all in her downpour
of power,
rushing forth in a massive
surge,
and coming from who knows where.
I know.
The past.

I lift my lids to see her eyes,
but she shuts them just in time.
She tilts her head
and breathes in deeply
in lovely, loving
nourishment.
And she is gone,
to bring it all back
here.

Quin-Shei

Sometimes I can taste lost love. It tastes like maple syrup dripping ever so slowly down the side of your mouth where your
tongue can almost reach it. It rolls down thickly, at a leisurely,
languid pace. Your mind goes crazy as you wait for the moment
when it reaches just that right spot, the place where your tongue
can barely reach it. But lost love is like a misanthrope. It doesn't
want to be tasted or cherished. It just slides down to a point where
your tongue strains and strains but just can't get to it. The only
way to taste lost love is when your voracious mind is wild with
desire and you imagine it. It makes you keep hoping and attempting until the alluring twinkle of the stars and the heavens come
down to meet you.

My grandmother, Quin-Shei, is the portrait of lost love, for
she can't come to terms with the fact that Poppa left her. I see her
mostly in the summertime and try to assuage the pain that glim-
mers in her eyes. Her feeble hands, wrinkled and parched, fumble
about the cluttered house as she talks to a husband who isn't
there. She sits on the balcony, gazing deeply into the ungiving,
star-filled welkin, and cries. I watch her as she rocks gently to
and fro, rubbing a flower against her face while she stares at the
moon. Sometimes she wraps a loose thread around and around
her finger until it becomes red and taut like a drop of blood. These
are the times when I see lost love shimmering amidst her whole
fragile being. These are the times when it feels as if she will never
be pacified.

On some nights I seat myself inside and watch her watching
the moon. I am swept with nostalgia as I remember Poppa. He
and Grandma were such a stately couple. Sitting on the balcony,
they'd sip their iced tea and hold hands. The cubes of ice bumping into each other, along with the polite sips of my grandpar-
ents, were the only sounds heard on many of those cool nights. I
can see this all in her eyes, for she remembers too.

The cool nights passed away, and our clothes began to stick
uncomfortably to our skin. We could feel the sun dripping down
our foreheads, making our faces swollen and moist. Poppa would
have these strange spells of malevolence, where flower pots broke,
picture frames flew through the air, and Grandma cried. Being
the patriarch, he could crack, throw and do all the doings of a
miscreant, and Grandma and I would sit silently and absorb.
These were the hotter nights, evenings of ancient passion swel-
tering to a point of sheer disbelief that anything outside the house
existed. Only our tight circle of burning pain and harm was real.

When he was gone, my relief was a humid summer day transforming itself into the clear, crisp night. I am happy that we are
extricated, freed from his wrath. My only pain now is having to
witness her lost love. I watch her. She sits silently on a hard,
wooden chair, rocking her body back and forth. The eyes seem

alert, and they seem to be waiting. I know what she is staring at. It isn't just the moon, the stars; it is the potency of her enduring love. Her eyes strain and then I see it. It is there, in the sky, and it is beckoning with all its sweet cunning. We can almost taste it.

Mey Yiok

In the summer she would wake up moist under the smoldering Philippine sun. Her youth was spent along the paved but broken roads of Paco, a district of Manila, with the rundown buses raising the heavy dust thick into the air. She saw her home as she saw all of the Philippines, a poor, broken, hot place. She was a girl who knew the heat well, for each day she worked and sweated in it, along with all that radiated from the family's bakery. Yes, heat and hard work were two things she was well acquainted with. They both wore her down, yet made her resilient. She grew up out of that heat, the broken roads, the dust; she became a strong, enduring woman before she moved from the Philippines. She became a woman of stamina, vitality, courage, yearning. She became all of these things, before she moved to America, and became my mother.

Her past seems so foreign to me that when she speaks of it I picture someone else in place of my mother. I see a young woman, strong and vibrant, the one that always smiles crooked in the black and white photos. She was the one who always looked a bit bashful and nervous, dark glasses sometimes hiding her eyes. I form this image as I hear my mother's voice carving out the figure, and I see this girl as I examine the faded pictures that spill out from her old and dusty shoebox.

"Why did you come here?" I asked her.

"Why? Your father come to school here. I marry him," she said simply. "I only sad because I miss my family. I had to leave them."

"What did you feel when you first entered America?" I asked. "Did you like it?"

She looked down and thought a moment. She rubbed the edge of the tablecloth between her thumb and forefinger. She bit her lip, and suddenly something came to her. She started smiling, then giggling, then she went into hysterical laughter. She squeezed her eyes shut, put her hand over her mouth but didn't make a sound. Her body just shook and jiggled with mirth.

"I learn . . . a . . . lot," she stuttered. "I did not know how to cook meat and I put *everything* in one washing machine. Cashmere sweater become . . . *this small!*" My mother could hardly stop laughing, and I sat there, listening to her belt out a couple of more stories about domestic problems. Finally she calmed down.

"Why? Why did you have so many problems?"

"Why?" Because . . . because we have many servants in the Philippines . . . many, many servants. Even the littlest thing I don't do. I come here and have to learn to do everything. I just work hard in bakery before. Very difficult . . . very, very hard."

She didn't really want to talk anymore. She had to prepare dinner and write out forms for her job at the bank. It wasn't until a couple of days later that the subject of her past came up again.

"You know how much money we had? One thousand dollars. We were very poor. Before, I could put my hand in bakery register and get money. Every week I had new dress . . . We come here, we really poor. Every week we ate a lot of gai-don (eggs), and we ate a lot of chicken. Sixty-nine cents for chicken."

"Chicken doesn't sound so bad," I tell her.

She looked at me.

"When you have no choice, then it's bad."

I looked down and felt ashamed. I've felt this before; she sometimes would stare at me critically as if I could never comprehend anything but my own life, my own experiences. I felt like a little child staring at my own murky reflection in a deep, deep pond.

My mother talked a little more about the adjustment to American life. She laughed as she told me how my brother used to get his head hurt all the time when her nervousness caused her to brake suddenly while driving, causing him to bang into the windshield. She grew laconic and quiet when she spoke of leaving her parents behind to enter into a new country with a new husband. I was unearthing old memories with my questions, and I could see the effect of sad, hard remembrances on her face. She nodded while she spoke, tightened her lips. Her eyes concentrated on something in the far-off distance and would rarely meet my own. Then the questioning suddenly ceased.

I watched her quick hands straighten out the photos on the table in a neat, rectangular pile. She stopped a moment, and stared at a picture of a young girl dressed in a white dress. Her hair was pulled back in pins and her dress hung loosely, billowing in the wind.

I thought I would never know this girl. I thought I would never connect her with my mother. To me she had seemed like separate person. This girl's hair was longer, more stringy, as if the moisture in the air was clinging to it. My mother's hair is neatly permed and cropped to frame her face. This girl's skin was flushed and smooth. My mother's face is dry with powder and foundation, little crevices edging their way around her eyes. The two pairs of eyes stare back at me, both saying the same thing: the past belonged to them; yet, as I sift through the hundreds of photographs and listen to the echoed memories, I slowly begin to understand.

Visions

I saw her today . . .
The one behind the tightened lips
Underneath the thin layers of
my life.
She wasn't mother.
She wasn't wife.
I didn't know she existed.

I saw her today.
A flash of red and gold
That glimmered just slightly
Behind the droop of her slanted eyes,
Beyond the soft suckle of my thumb,
Beyond my own infantile cries,
I had drunk her milk and closed my eyes.

I saw her today.
She smelt of tea and grassy fields.
It had clung to her in a tight embrace
For only what seemed
Like a fleeting moment,
Until a dab of perfume took its place.
Didn't she always smell so nice?

This girl I see,
Dancing with butterflies and
Unforgotten orchids,
Not so tense, not so wise,
With the glowing shine
Of a Golden Buddha.

They stare back at me,
Their eyes reflecting mine.

Rubric for Assessing the Reflective Essay

In assessing the reflective essay, we need to look not only at the specific characteristics of this kind of writing, but also for the more generic qualities of good writing: coherence, style, and use of standard conventions (see pages 84–85). *Coherence* is demonstrated to readers through emphasis, organization, logic, and repetition achieved through recurrences of language, syntax, and ideas. *Style,* for the purposes of this rubric, is observable in two written language features: (1) *sentence control,* and (2) *word choice* or *diction*. In assessment of the effectiveness of style, the primary considerations are *appropriateness, precision,* and *control*.

Reflective Essay Rubric Using a 5-Point Scale

Strategies	Score Point 5	Score Point 4	Score Point 3	Score Point 2	Score Point 1
Occasion for Reflection: a thing seen, read, or experienced Strategies for presentation: ■ description using concrete language and sensory detail ■ narrative strategies such as pacing, dialogue, action ■ citation giving location of original quotation or subject ■ web of related, parallel commentaries that serve as the occasion	**Occasion for Reflection: a thing seen, read, or experienced** ■ presents an extended occasion with rich detail ■ grounds the essay by describing an animal, object, quotation, or experience ■ using language rich in sensory detail ■ recording specific behaviors, properties, or actions ■ using narrative or anecdotal strategies such as pacing, dialogue, action ■ citing quotation or specific instance as the basis for reflection	**Occasion for Reflection: a thing seen, read, or experienced** ■ presents an extended, concrete occasion ■ grounds the essay by describing an animal, object, quotation, or experience ■ using sensory detail ■ recording behaviors, properties, or actions ■ using narrative or anecdotal strategies such as dialogue and action ■ citing the basis for reflection	**Occasion for Reflection: a thing seen, read, or experienced** ■ presents a concrete occasion at least briefly or ■ presents a concrete occasion that dominates the essay ■ grounds the essay by describing an animal, object, or experience ■ using some sensory detail ■ using narrative strategies	**Occasion for Reflection: a thing seen, read, or experienced** ■ presents an occasion or ■ presents an example chosen to illustrate a generalization already determined ■ uses some detail, often of a general nature ■ often uses narrative in the "telling" rather than "showing" mode	**Occasion for Reflection: a thing seen, read, or experienced** ■ there may be no stated occasion or the occasion may dominate the essay ■ often tells an autobiographical story rather than presenting an occasion
Reflection Possibilities for reflection: ■ extended exploration of subject ■ explicit, insightful generalizations or ■ implicit, embedded generalization based on extended narration	**Reflection** ■ engages in extended, thoughtful, perceptive reflections ■ moves from personal to general reflections ■ has sense of discovery or deepening insights	**Reflection** ■ engages in thoughtful reflections ■ moves from personal to general reflections ■ has some sense of discovery or deepened insights	**Reflection** ■ engages in reflective thinking, often in a predictable or commonplace way ■ has personal reflections ■ moves to at least a brief general reflection	**Reflection** ■ may rely on personal reflection to the exclusion of general reflection ■ often has a meandering rather than purposefully exploratory quality ■ often has a moralistic conclusion	**Reflection** ■ may be brief and simplistic, often leaning toward statements of belief or opinion rather than reflection ■ reflection may not be present at all

Reflective Essay Rubric Using a 5-Point Scale continued

Coherence, Style, and Conventions	Coherence, Style, and Conventions	Coherence, Style, and Conventions	Coherence, Style, and Conventions	Coherence, Style, and Conventions	Coherence, Style, and Conventions
Coherence Style: ■ diction ■ sentence structure Conventions: ■ uses standard English mechanics, spelling, and usage	Coherence: ■ has a logical, organic organization Style: ■ diction: uses language with imagination, precision, and appropriateness ■ sentence structure shows control and variety for effect Conventions: ■ uses standard English mechanics, spelling, and usage with few, if any, lapses in correctness	Coherence: ■ has a logical organization Style: ■ diction: uses language with appropriateness ■ sentence structure shows control and variety for effect Conventions: ■ uses standard English mechanics, spelling, and usage with some lapses in correctness	Coherence: ■ has a logical organization Style: ■ diction: uses language with appropriateness ■ shows control of basic sentence structures Conventions: ■ uses standard English mechanics, spelling, and usage with some lapses in correctness	Coherence: ■ may lapse in coherence or may be organized as a simple narrative Style: ■ diction: language is often general rather than specific ■ shows control of basic sentence structures Conventions: ■ uses standard English mechanics, spelling, and usage with frequent lapses in correctness	Coherence: ■ may lapse in coherence or may be organized as a simple narrative Style: ■ diction: language is often general rather than specific ■ may show control of basic sentence structures or ■ may have serious problems with basic sentence structures Conventions: ■ generally has frequent lapses in correctness

Appendix: Classroom Resources for Reflective Essays

Reflective essays may be found in numerous publications including newspapers and magazines. Most novels contain reflective sections. Teachers will want to have a large selection in the classroom library of works, particularly essays and poems, that contain reflective writing and that generate ideas for reflective essays. For starters, these particular texts are rich both in reflective pieces and in ideas to generate reflective essays:

A useful text might be *Learning the Landscape: Inquiry-Based Activities for Comprehending and Composing*, by Fran Claggett, Louann Reid, and Ruth Vinz. This book contains the foundation for the field notes activities, as well as an extended analysis of a Loren Eiseley essay, student illustrations, field notes from naturalists, and additional reflective essays and poems.

Individual essays and poems that work well are listed below.

Ackerman, Diane. *A Natural History of the Senses*. New York: Vintage, 1991.

Bly, Robert, ed. *News of the Universe: Poems of Twofold Consciousness*. 1980. San Francisco: Sierra Club, 1995.

Didion, Joan. *Slouching toward Bethlehem* New York: Farrar, 1968.

Dillard, Annie. "Death of a Moth." *Recasting the Text: Inquiry-Based Activities for Comprehending and Composing*. Ed. Fran Claggett, Louann Reid, and Ruth Vinz. Portsmouth, NH: Heinemann, 1996. 238–41.

———. *Pilgrim at Tinker Creek*. 1974. New York: Harper, 1998.

———. *Teaching a Stone to Talk: Expeditions and Encounters*. New York: Harper, 1982.

Lightman, Alan: *Einstein's Dreams: A Novel*. New York: Warner, 1993.

Lopez, Barry. *Crossing Open Ground*. New York: Vintage, 1978.

Rosenberg, Liz, ed. *Earth-Shattering Poems*. New York: Holt, 1998.

Stine, Annie, ed. *Contemporary Writers Celebrate the Landscapes of Home*. San Francisco: Sierra Club, 1996.

Thoreau, Henry David. *Walden*. 1854. Princeton: Princeton UP, 1989.

———. *Civil Disobedience and Other Essays*. New York: Dover, 1993.

Woolf, Virginia. "The Death of the Moth." *Recasting the Text: Inquiry-Based Activities for Comprehending and Composing*. Fran Claggett, Louann Reid, and Ruth Vinz. Portsmouth, NH: Heinemann, 1996. 246–48.

7 Memoir

Memory is the mother of all wisdom.
>   Aeschylus

We don't remember days; we remember moments.
>   Cesare Pavese

The past is what you remember, imagine you remember, convince yourself you remember, or pretend you remember.
>   Harold Pinter

The word *memoir*, according to the Oxford English Dictionary, refers to "a record of events, not purporting to be a complete history, but treating of such matters as come within the personal knowledge of the writer, or are obtained from a certain particular source of information." This definition separates it clearly from the concept of autobiography, which generally encompasses whole lives, or at least larger, focused parts of lives. No autobiography can, in fact, tell the story of an entire life, so it too is, in effect, a series of memoirs. In autobiography, the writer is usually concerned with the chronology of a life, whereas in memoir, the writer generally uses narrative to depict small moments in his or her life, then move to reflection on some aspect of that life—ideas, events, or relationships. Memoir is the medium of life stories, stories that we share with friends and family. As a genre of writing, however, it becomes more consciously literary, with careful attention to the artistic or stylistic elements that presume an audience beyond intimates.

It is important to note that the memoir has become more and more important to the general reading public; browsing among the new books in the library reveals a preponderance of memoirs. A look at the schedule of classes in any community college or extended education program will show the popularity of memoir classes. In addition, there are a number of online memoir classes for all age groups, showing the popularity of "telling one's story."

Features of the Memoir

Peter Gilmour, in his illuminating book *The Wisdom of Memoir*, writes: "One consistent dynamic undergirds the varied forms and styles of memoir: recollection of a given experience, reflection on that experience, and communication of the reflected experience. Memory recalls experience. Concentration, focus, perspective, comparison, and contrast fuel the reflection. Communication of reflected experience relies on verbal skills—either oral or written—a sense of audience, and a willingness to share personally significant events and their meaning. This energy culminates in an artistic form—an icon—that embodies and expresses experience and reflection on experience" (91).

Isolating these features, then, we can list the characteristics of the written memoir genre as follows:

- *recollection* of an event or experience
- *reflection* of that experience to show its meaning for the writer
- *communication* of the experience through writing for a particular audience

The memoir will use the strategies typical of narrative (concrete language depicting action, remembered or created dialogue, clear description) as well as reflection (moving from the immediate or personal to the generalized or distanced significance). The stylistic or artistic aspects of memoir give it form, in this case an organic form rising from the nature of the particular piece.

While the memoir includes a range of kinds of writing, from the informal diary or slightly less informal journal to the personal essay that incorporates a narrative, one feature is constant: the narrator of the memoir is the "I" of the piece. One can, of course, write a fictional memoir, but even so, the narrator will take the persona of the "I."

Teaching Activities for the Memoir

There are as many ways to approach the teaching of the memoir as there are kinds of memoirs. Most teachers have taught memoir under various guises—autobiographical incident, personal essay, vignette—and have their own approaches to this kind of writing. What we present here is the framework for any number of memoir assignments: the Lifeline. This framework has been used in hundreds of classrooms with both middle school and high school students as well as with adults in teacher workshops and extended education classes. It provides the teacher with the flexibility to design literally dozens of assignments.

Following are instructions for generating the Lifeline, then suggestions for a number of specific memoir assignments using the Lifeline.

Making the Lifeline

Materials needed are a large sheet of paper and thin colored markers or pencils. To make the chart, have students follow these steps:

- Take a full sheet of binder paper (or use a file folder) and turn it sideways.
- Make vertical lines, enough to represent their current age. Each line on their paper represents one year.
- At the bottom of the page, number each line. These lines stand for their age.
- Draw a horizontal line about 1 ½ inches from the top, creating a top border. They will use the space at the top for identifying places and events.
- Draw a horizontal line dividing the remaining space. This is the valence line. They will use this line when they enter their relationships.

The Vertical Lines

Places

Have students record all the places they have lived by a drawing a vertical line for each one at the appropriate age. They should use one color for all places, and use the top border space to record the name of the place.

Note: A *place* may be a house, a city, a country. Students may include places they have visited that were significant as well as places where they actually lived.

Events

Have students think about stepping-stones, passages, epiphanies, pets, holidays, vacations, births, deaths, and then record selected events by drawing a vertical line for each one at the appropriate age. They should use a second color for all events. In the space at the top, have them jot down a word or phrase that will enable them to recall the event at a later time.

The Horizontal Lines

The Relationship Lines

Students should first have drawn the valence line to indicate the median, or a neutral relationship. Next they choose three or more people who have been important in their lives. Using a different color for each person, they draw a *horizontal* line that moves above and below the valence line to show how they felt about each person at each age of their lives. (Begin with a dot to indicate when the person entered the writer's life. If a person has died, use a dotted line to indicate the continued influence of this person in his or her life. If a person is no longer important at all, use a large dot to indicate the end of the relationship.)

The Self Line

This line represents them and how they have felt about themselves during their lives. They should choose a color to represent them and draw a horizontal line using the valence line as their neutral reference point.

The Major-Interest Line

Have students think about a major interest in their lives—a strong interest in an idea, thing, activity, place. It might be as pervasive as the power of art, of music, of a particular sport. It might be an interest in something like birds, whales, wolves. It might be a preoccupation with living near the ocean or with saving the planet.

Have students trace a horizontal line, using the valence line as their neutral reference point, indicating when this interest first appeared, when it was a major force in their lives, when it receded, where it is now.

Writings That Stem from a Study of the Lifeline

There are innumerable opportunities for memoir pieces from the lifeline. The *zenith-nadir writings*, however, are provocative and productive starting points.

The Zenith Paper

Ask students to select the zenith (the high point or one of the high points) of the self line; this should be a moment when they felt capable of being who they want to be, of being able to do anything successfully. Look at the "slice of life" where it occurs: e.g., where were they, what was going on in their lives, how they felt about other people, etc. Then have them *choose one moment from this slice and record the moment*, writing freely.

Their goal next is to refine the writing. They should look for ways to hone, cut, make this piece as precise and elegant as possible. Try having them think in terms of a vignette, a short memoir with dramatic intent. They might use dialogue to set the stage, but that is not necessary. The final paper may be only one page long if they have been successful in writing just the moment.

The Nadir Paper

When students have finished the zenith papers, they go through the same process with a nadir moment. Interestingly, many students find the "nadir paper," as they call it, the most important piece of writing they have done to this point. We should mention that in classes that have used these two assignments, students invariably want them included in their final class assessment portfolios. The zenith paper and the nadir paper together may become the genesis of a portfolio of memoirs, vignettes derived from studying the lifeline.

Additional Memoir Possibilities

Each of the lines itself offers a number of possible topics:

- Have students look at their place lines and select the places that most influenced them as children. Write a "Where I'm From" poem using elements from this place—people, foods, descriptions of the place itself, things that they associate with the place. (The poem "Where I'm From," by George Ella Lyon, in her *Where I'm From, Where Poems Come From* [Spring, TX: Absey, 1999] is a good starter for this activity.)

- Again looking at their place lines, students should write about the place that is most important to them. Ask them to figure out why, then write about the place. They may begin with a description of the place, then move to implications.

Students might also consider the major-interest line:

- Identify the origin of their major interests. Trace their influence on their lives: how have their interests influenced, for instance, their choice of friends, how they spend their time, what they plan to do with their lives, where they might live in the future.

- Have them choose one moment, one incident that reveals their interest in this idea, thing, activity, place. Write this moment.

Now ask students to look at the events line and identify something that resulted from a choice they made, then do the following:

- Write about the effects of this choice. Explore the reasons they acted as they did, or the reasons the event happened as it did, or the reasons it affected them as it did.

- Think about what might have happened had they made a different choice, then write this alternative choice as if it were an event that happened.

- Have students choose one pivotal event that has to do with shaping their values and write this event, considering the other people involved, then reflect on how this event has helped shape their present values.

Ask students to look at the relationship lines, then:

- Consider one of their relationship lines. Write a study of their relationship with this person. Choose one or more moments that show this relationship. Write, then reflect on the impact, positive and/or negative, that this relationship has had on them and their lives.
- In other relationship ideas, they might:
  - ◆ Write about a moment when they discovered that a particular person was truly a friend.
  - ◆ Write about a moment when they discovered that someone they thought was a friend was not.

The self line:

- Have students consider the shape of their "self" lines and explore their perceptions of the path that their lives have taken/are taking. Here they may draw on any aspect of the lifeline—places, events, relationships, major interest—that is appropriate.

Most teachers like to use the memoir at various points during the year, either as stand-alone assignments or as adjuncts to various works of literature. Poems, for example, often lend themselves to topics for memoirs, which can be either prose or poetry.

Self-Assessment

This assessment may be applied to a single memoir assignment or to an entire project, one that resulted in a memoir booklet.

Give students about twenty minutes in class to write a self-assessment essay in which they evaluate their processes and participation in writing their memoir. Emphasize that this is first-draft writing, but they should write it as an essay rather than as answers to specific questions you might suggest. You might ask them to consider such questions as:

- How much effort did you put into this project?
- How do you feel about your final product—aside from the relief of having it finally completed?
- Where do you see improvement in your writing? Where do you still want to work on your writing?
- How much energy did you put into your work with your group? How did you benefit from it? If you did not benefit from this

part of the process, why? (Because you hadn't completed the assignment as well as you might have, or because your group was not effective?)

The Read-Around

Collect the memoirs and put them on a table toward the front of the room. Distribute packets of self-stick notes. Students should use the remainder of their time reading, enjoying, and responding to the writings of their classmates. Ask students to write a short response to each paper they read. At the end of the period, have students find their papers and read the responses before handing them in.

Assessing the Memoir

The primary question for assessing any piece of writing should be "How well does this piece of writing fulfill the purposes of the writer?" In the case of memoir, we can look at the purposes embodied in the features of the genre as we set them forth in the beginning, that a memoir involves these characteristics:

- memory of an event or experience (recollection)
- reflection on that experience to show its meaning for the writer
- communication of the experience through writing for a particular audience

Beyond those features, the completed memoir has an artistic form that embodies and expresses the experience, the reflection, and the communication of that experience. The achievement of artistic form may be assessed by looking carefully at the intended audience and noting whether the communication was successful.

We hope you will urge students to see that their memoirs reach their intended audiences, whether those audiences are individuals or larger groups of people, members of their families or readers of the school or community newspaper, for example. There are also a number of magazines that publish the work of young people; a look at the *Writer's Market* for the current year will provide names of publications, editors' names, and addresses.

Student Memoir

The following memoir was written by Adam Dumas when he was a student at Portland Middle School, Portland, Michigan. His teacher was Nancy Patterson, who wrote Chapter 11, "Integrating Computers into the Writing Classroom." Adam's paper shows the strength of precise language, rich detail, and meaningful organization. This memoir depicts an important time in Adam's adolescence and shows the bond between father and son that developed during the process of building "Adam's Tree House."

Memoir: A Journey into Your Past
Adam's Tree House

I never thought that I would have something so cool that I would be the envy of the neighborhood. I never thought that I would have something so cool that parents would take their kids for walks past our house every once and a while just to see it. I never thought I would have a convenient place in our backyard to be by myself or hang out with others and be left alone for a while, until now. Adam's tree house was built in the summer and fall of 1998.

It started in May of 1998. We moved into the house around the corner from our original house that we had lived in since we first came to Portland. I was amazed at the size and beauty of our new house. As I gave myself a tour I noticed our backyard. I stepped out our back door into the hot rays of the sun. The water in our new pool never looked better and the woods in our backyard sprung many ideas of fun into my mind. It was a great feeling to know that this is the house that I will live in all my teen years. Then I noticed the tree in our backyard. At that time I didn't know why, but when I looked at the tree I immediately thought of building some small stand or maybe a tree house up in the tree.

As soon as we moved completely into our house, I began to love to climb the tree and see how high I could get. My mom would get extremely worried that I would fall and she would limit how high I could go. But being up so high was exciting for me. The feeling of adrenalin as I looked over our house was really amazing. The way that this tree grew made it easy to climb. Being up high gave me a new view on the neighborhood.

After we sold our first house and unpacked our belongings, my dad mentioned that my favorite climbing tree would be perfect for a tree house. He explained to me that the way the limbs of the tree formed a fair sized cup was in the perfect position to lay boards down and build a floor. Of course I agreed and for the rest of the year until winter we decided to make a father and son project up in the tree.

To start the project we had to order a lot of wood to build the floor. We took several trips to and from the lumberyard until we had all the wood we needed. When we started building the floor, I thought it was really cool how my dad formed a grid similar to a large tic-tac-toe board to create a sturdy floor. One problem was that we had to build around a tree trunk going vertically through one side of the floor. Even though the tree was perfect for the job, we still had to build around many tree limbs. Finally, through many different tricky footing positions, and through many troubles with tools, we finished the floor with special floor paint.

My dad studied carpentry in college and taught building trades once he got his teaching certificate. He was a licensed builder and did many odd jobs to bring in extra money before he went into administration. My dad has always been handy around the house. He fixed the plumbing as my mom fixed dinner. He fixed the television as my mom went to the grocery story. Dad is a member of the Handy Man Club of America. He has every little tool and has saved a lot of people a lot of money by helping them work. My dad has a lot of history with building and making little projects.

After many more trips to and from the lumberyard again, we started on the walls. The rough wood slipped slivers into my hands as I strained to haul piles of 2 x 4's into our garage. We laid out the wood on the garage floor forming the basic studs for the four walls. We built the walls in the garage because it would be way too hard to build eight by eight walls on an eight by eight floor ten feet up in a tree. We nailed the frame together and left room for a door in one wall, and windows in another two walls. My dad received windows from a friend because they remodeled their house.

To get the walls up in the tree, we used a pulley system. This was my favorite part of building the tree house because we got the whole family involved! I climbed up the tree and tied a pulley system wheel to a tree limb with a chain. We then ran a rope through the wheel and tied one end to the wall, the other end to the lawn mower. Using the twelve horsepower engine on the mower, we slowly but surely pulled the rope around the wheel and lifted the four walls off the ground and into place. It wasn't until we had every wall screwed and nailed down firmly that we attached the wood siding to the studs.

We took another trip to the lumberyard to get sheets of wood for the siding. Most people think that you could just cut the siding to size and nail it right to the studs. But it wasn't that easy for my dad and me. We actually had two tree limbs to build around and one went directly through the tree house. This was the hardest part of building Adam's tree house. First we measured the width of the two limbs just to get a basic measurement. Then we had to cut as close as we could to the exact shape of the tree limb. After we managed to tackle that problem, the other walls were pretty easy.

I guess Mr. Handyman, my dad of course, got a little carried away with a tree house. You could actually see a house forming in a tree. I was expecting just a floor with a railing like you might see in the movies. We would be outside from morning to night some days, either just enjoying it or working on it to make it better. We ate lunch on a small table one afternoon in the tree house as my dad was filling the cracks between the tree and the walls. We spent some good father and son time that we spent up in the tree house.

After we had all four walls set and perfect, we constructed a roof in the garage. By this time, I wasn't scared to climb the ninety-degree walls to help bring the wall into place, but my big brother was! All my friends from the neighborhood wanted to help put finishing touches on the tree house. It was so cool to hang out on the roof of the tree house and nail the shingles on firmly.

III Strategies for Teaching Writing

When studying the work of the masters,
    I watch the working of their minds.

Surely, facility with language
    and the charging of the word with energy

are effects that can be achieved
    by various means.

                The Art of Writing: Lu Chi's Wen Fu

This section moves from a study of genre to an examination of various strategies that we can use in teaching writing.

Chapter 8 presents a number of strategies for teaching the craft and the art of poetry, often the least taught of the major kinds of writing. We place it here rather than in the genre section because poetry encompasses the range of genres within its umbrella status, from telling a story to describing the natural world to attempting to persuade to reflecting on one's experience.

Chapter 9, "Learning Writing Strategies through Modeling," describes a number of kinds of modeling that can be integrated into teaching any of the genres.

Chapter 10, by contributing author Louann Reid, presents an innovative look at ways to teach grammar in contexts for writing. For decades, teachers have struggled with how to teach grammar in a way that has some carryover value for teaching writing. Dr. Reid presents valuable insights into strategies that actually can affect student writing.

Chapter 11, by contributing author Nancy Patterson, brings us well into the twenty-first century with some concrete strategies for integrating computers into the writing classroom. Dr. Patterson gives examples, as well, demonstrating work from middle school students.

8 Poetry: The Craft and the Art

A writing program without poetry is a body without bones, without eyes, without hands. Poetry gives shape, form, and strength to language; it gives images to ideas.

Fran Claggett, from "Poetry as a Window into Culture"

Poetry in the average classroom is in a precarious state. Although more teachers than ever are reading poems with their students, sharing a poem-a-day, or encouraging young poets to post their poems on the Internet, poetry is still either ignored or taught for the wrong reasons in thousands of classrooms. Because it is not one of the kinds of writing that are part of the large-scale testing bureaucracy, it too often gets dropped from the curriculum for what many teachers see as their critical function: teaching the kinds of writing that students will have to produce on tests.

It is an easy out for those teachers who remember only the frustrating analytic poetry assignments from their school days and are not comfortable with poetry themselves. In a recent workshop of over a hundred teachers, four out of five had taught no poetry during that school year. This was in February. They admittedly felt guilty about it but didn't think they had the time or personal resources to teach it well. What often passes for teaching poetry in test-driven classrooms is teaching *about* poetry: the definitions of "poetic devices," kinds of poems, structural elements. These are the things that can easily be tested. To base a poetry program on these limited approaches, however, does a great disservice to students who, given the right motivation, will not only become readers of poetry but also writers.

Despite poetry-deprived classrooms, poetry continues to thrive in our culture. In many communities poets crowd the mikes in coffee houses in weekly gatherings. Small towns and big cities are naming poets laureate to foster the love of poetry. Ted Kooser and Billy Collins, recent poets laureate of the United States, have made it a priority to encourage the reading and writing of poetry in schools.

"But I can't add another thing to my curriculum!"

How many times have we heard this comment when we're talking about the need to include poetry in the classroom? The problem is with the word *add*. Of course there is no room to *add* anything, but there is always room to rearrange things to make better use of the time we do have. Our contention is that poetry should be a given in our classrooms.

- No other kind of writing provides as many rich opportunities for learning both the *art and the craft* of *reading and writing.*
- Poetry is basic to improving both reading and writing skills, no matter the level of the learner, whether struggling or advanced.
- Students naturally are drawn to poetry, even if you have to get over the traditional lament of "hating poetry," which is more a ritualistic response than a genuine feeling.

In classrooms where poetry is evident on the walls, in classroom libraries, in students' hands, the reading and writing of poetry provides a central function. Students who begin as writers of poems soon begin thinking of themselves as poets, and find it natural to read the kind of literature they themselves are writing. Teachers in these classrooms encourage students to engage in such practices as reading aloud, using others' poems as springboards for their own, constructing graphics, exploring craft, and learning about poets' lives. Students learn to interweave their reading and writing, gaining inspiration from reading one another's poems as well as those of established writers. What a contrast to the classroom where the only evidence of poetry is that assigned from a very large anthology as part of a lesson, often without context.

Poetry breaks down barriers: A poem written by a student who never wrote a word before she wrote that poem is posted on the wall next to one written by a student going to Stanford in the fall. These students read each other's poems and gain new appreciation for each other. Many students now go regularly to various sites on the Internet to post their own poems or read poems posted by others. By posting their poems, they complete the central purpose for writing: communication. Writer and reader meet in cyberspace.

For students with reading and writing problems, poems provide the ideal medium to help students learn critical reading and writing strategies. By using short poems, either narratives or lyrics, we engage them quickly with subjects that are central to their lives; we enable them to see the thing whole rather than in parts. Brain research tells us that people with a strongly developed right hemisphere learn better when they can hold a "whole" in their visual field at once. With students who learn in this holistic way, such short poems are ideal; students do not have to turn the page and lose what they have just gained. They see the whole poem at once and can attend to its structure and meaning much more easily than they could if they were reading a story or a novel or even a much longer poem. The best part is that reading and writing strategies learned with short poems carry over into longer works.

Writing poetry also provides contextual opportunities to teach revision and editing strategies as students prepare their poems for publication, whether within the classroom, on the Web, or in the world of contests, newspapers, and magazines. These factors, too, carry over when students are revising essays or research projects.

We strongly urge teachers to make the reading and the writing of poetry a constant presence in their curricula. While you will probably want to focus on poetry in a separate unit from time to time, we support the practice of many teachers who read or post a poem a day, a practice begun and supported by former laureate Billy Collins with his Poetry 180, as described on the Library of Congress Web site at www. loc.gov/poetry/180/. By interspersing poems by published writers with student poems, and simply reading (or having a student read), this practice takes little time. Through this constant reinforcement, allowing the poem to exert its own influence, students become familiar with the rhythms and cadences of the language without having to "find the hidden meaning" in each poem.

We also support times when you ask students to engage in the deep study of a poem, to learn what happens when a poem opens up after intense study. When poetry is vital in a variety of ways in the classroom, students learn they can read and enjoy poetry on their own, and, perhaps, as our students do, take over that mike in the local coffeehouse on open poetry reading night.

In summary, poetry gives students

- power and control in working with language: word, phrase, sentence
- joy in both reading and creating images that replicate what we have seen, tasted, heard, touched
- knowledge and facility with the way language presents opportunities to depict images, create metaphors, construct ideas
- understanding of how meanings spiral from level to level

Features of Poetry

In attempting to write about the features of poetry, we are led by necessity to attempt a definition of poetry itself. In her famous essay "Poetry and Grammar," Gertrude Stein once asked, "What is poetry and if you know what poetry is what is prose" (209). This question alone is enough for a good discussion. Everyone has an opinion of what poetry is, and definitions, even by poets, range widely over the poetic landscape.[1]

As starters for class discussion, you might give students these two forms of a piece written by Dawn Thomas when she was a high school senior:

Form A

On Being a Senior

Suddenly all the juice flowed out of me, staining the floor. I sit on my hard plastic seat, information flying around, wondering who I will lunch with. Brrrrrrrrrrrhm. Smile stamped on, I float to my next class, leafing through a *Mademoiselle;* more stamped smiles. I fly out the window and I'm free, running around on blue skied grass. Brrrrrrhm. Madly, I copy questions, the teacher winks. This room has shrunk over the last four years. In my book, names I've watched grow old Go off to College. I sit struggling in my High School skin; detestable thing! I will endure. I leave a strip of skin behind, and, and move to the next class.

Form B

On Being a Senior

Suddenly all the juice flowed out of me,
Staining the floor.
I sit on my hard plastic seat,
Information flying around,
Wondering who I will lunch with.
Brrrrrrrrrrrhm.
Smile stamped on,
I float to my next class,
Leafing through a *Mademoiselle;*
More stamped smiles.
I fly out the window and I'm free,
Running around on blue skied grass.
Brrrrrrhm.
Madly, I copy questions,
The teacher winks.
This room has shrunk over the last four years.
In my book, names I've watched grow old
Go off to College.
I sit struggling in my High School skin;
Detestable thing!
Brrrrrrhm.
I will endure.
I leave a strip of skin behind,
And, and move to the next class.

Have students discuss these two presentations of the same words. Ask students to list the elements that make Form A a piece of prose, then list the elements that make Form B a piece of poetry. Finally, have them comment on whether "On Being a Senior" is more effective as prose or as poetry.

If you follow the method of having students wrestle with a genre before reading or studying about it, you could have students discuss these questions:

- What is poetry?
- What poems can they remember having read?
- How does poetry differ from other kinds of literature?
- What kind of people read poetry?
- What kind of people write poetry?

Poets on Poetry

Stein writes,

> Poetry is I say essentially a vocabulary just as prose is essentially not.
>
> And what is the vocabulary of which poetry absolutely is. It is a vocabulary based on the noun as prose is essentially and determinately and vigorously not based on the noun.
>
> Poetry is concerned with using with abusing, with losing with wanting, with denying with avoiding with adoring with replacing the noun. It is doing that always doing that, doing that and doing nothing but that. Poetry is doing nothing but using losing refusing and pleasing and betraying and caressing nouns. That is what poetry does, that is what poetry has to do no matter what kind of poetry it is. And there are a great many kinds of poetry. [. . . .]
>
> And so that is poetry really loving the name of anything and that is not prose. (231–32)

You might read that aloud to your students just to have them hear the fluid sounds of Stein!

Babette Deutsch writes, more traditionally, that poetry is the art that uses words "to reveal the realities that the senses record, the feelings salute, the mind perceives, and the shaping imagination orders" (110–12). Laurence Perrine and Thomas Arp, in their perpetually best-selling book *Sound and Sense*, take a similar position: "Poetry, finally, is a kind of multidimensional language. Ordinary language—the kind that we use to communicate information—is one-dimensional. [. . .] Its one dimension is intellectual. Poetry, which is language used to communicate experience, has at least four dimensions. If it is to communicate experience, it must be directed at the *whole* person, not just at your understanding. It must involve not only your intelligence but also your senses, emotions, and imagination" (9).

In a sentence that seems to foreshadow Marshall McLuhan's "the medium is the message," Wordsworth remarked that "the matter always comes out of the manner." This view of the interrelationship of content and form is one we will revisit later in this chapter.

To attempt to describe the features of poetry, then, is to make these assertions, knowing, as we have seen, that poetry is a fluid genre that can be defined in many ways:

- Purpose: to communicate experience
- Goal: to convey that experience through language that makes use of the rich resources of poetry
- Resources include connotation, imagery, metaphor, symbol, paradox, irony, allusion, sound repetition, rhythm, and pattern

Learning the Art and Craft of Poetry

Learning the craft of poetry is infinitely more manageable than learning the art. As English teachers, we commonly expect our students to read sonnets and other formally constructed poems, but we rarely assign the writing of them. Our position here, as with all the other genres we present, is that our best understanding occurs when we enter from the inside, when we not only read but write within the form we are studying. To that end, then, we offer suggestions for having students write haiku, sonnets, villanelles, and even sestinas. We hope you will not shy away from introducing these forms, along with the free verse that is the dominant contemporary kind of poetry.

In this book, we will present three ways of incorporating the writing of poems into the curriculum:

- in relation to the study of literature,
- in a writing workshop, and
- in using established forms.

I. Writing Poems in Relation to Literature

In Chapter 9, "Learning Writing Strategies through Modeling," you will find explanations and directions for teaching a range of formats for modeling poetry. We will not repeat those in this chapter, but urge you to incorporate modeling practices in your curriculum. In addition to modeling, there are many other possibilities of using literature to create new poems. We offer two here, one very simple and the other more complex.

The "Found-in-Literature" Poem

One way of incorporating the writing of poetry with the study of literature is the "found-in-literature poem." When you are reading a novel or short story, or even a long poem, ask students to select words and phrases from the text to create a poem of their own. They can alter placement and leave out words in sentences, but they must not add any words of their own. Even this short exercise leads students to read the original text very carefully.

Here is a poem from words and phrases found in Annie Dillard's essay "Death of a Moth." Even the title comes from the essay.

Reading a Novel about Rimbaud

I think I know moths,
The flames that move light
The color of skin.

Gold cat,
Barred owl,
A spider: moth-essence.

Is this what we live for?
Is this the only final beauty?

Parapoetics

Parapoetics is the art of creating new poems from words, phrases, and lines taken directly from two or more already-existing poems. Creating these hybrids, which students sometimes call "mutt poems," provides opportunities for students to read, relate to, and extract from, resulting in continually changing versions of the originals. These hybrid poems, containing elements of two or more "pedigreed" poems, reflect their origins but take on characteristics of their own.

Poems can be paired in different ways for this exercise: you may find two or three poems dealing with the same subject; you may choose poems from different time periods; or you may have students select the poems they want to work with.

It is useful for the teacher to select two poems to begin with and work through the process as a class; then have students work in pairs on additional sets. We generally select several sets of poems, giving students the option of selecting one of our sets or making another. One set that is very popular and is easily available is made up of two already-related poems: "I Hear America Singing," by Walt Whitman, and "I, Too, Sing America," by Langston Hughes. In this exercise it is interesting to note how different pairs of students focus on different elements of the two poems, coming up with very different-looking hybrids.

Directions

- With a partner, read both poems in the set you have chosen. Talk about what each poem is saying. Who is the speaker? What is she or he saying? How are the two poems related?

- Each of you should take responsibility for one of the poems, but talk together as you work. Underline or highlight words, phrases, lines that stand out for you.

- From these two "pedigreed" poems, create a "mutt poem" that conveys the essences of each of the poems, but results in a completely new poem.

   - Make two columns, one for each of the two poems.

   - Write words, phrases, or complete lines from the two poems, each in the appropriate column so that, when you read them in two voices, they make a new kind of sense.

   - You may use repetition, you may vary the order in which the words appear, but use only the words of the two poems in your final poem.

   - Read the new poem with your partner as a dialogue, each reading the words from one of the poems.

Here is an example of a poem created from these two poems, Whitman's lines on the left margin, Hughes's indented:

I hear America singing
   I, too, sing America
Mechanics, carpenter, mason, boatman
   I am the darker brother
I hear America singing
   I, too, sing America
Mechanics, carpenter, mason, boatman
   I am the darker brother
Deckhand, shoemaker singing
   They send me to eat in the kitchen
The mother, the wife, the girl sewing or washing
   But I laugh, and eat well
The day what belongs to the day
   Tomorrow, I'll be at the table
   when company comes

> Singing with open mouths
> > They'll see how beautiful I am
> > I, too, am America
> I hear American singing

As a follow-up to the exercise, ask students to discuss how their understanding of these two poems was affected by the process of making a new poem from the two poems in their set. Did it change? If so, how? You might want students to write a journal entry or a short paper commenting on the process as well as on their understanding of the two poems.

Note: A related kind of poetry writing is the *paralogue,* which is described in the next chapter, on modeling.

II. Writing Poems in Writing Workshop

Teachers have many ways of structuring a writing-workshop classroom. We like to introduce students to many different options in how to approach the writing of poems. We like to see a classroom filled with books of poetry, especially small books written by individual authors or books dealing with one theme. (Paul Janeczko's collections are particularly useful for thematic poems that appeal to teenagers.) Students should be free to read during the poetry writing workshop as well as write.

You might want to spend ten minutes or so at the beginning of each workshop class introducing either a particular kind of poem or a function of poetry, such as metaphor or concrete images, giving students suggestions for their reading or writing. After a week or so, limit the introductions to a couple of times a week, giving students more time to try things out. Even students who have their own agendas will profit from seeing some alternatives, even as they pursue their own work. Poetic terms that could be used in whole-class introductions include simile, metaphor, symbol, figurative language, and personification. Metric and stanza terminology is best saved for specific use as students need it.

Following are some kinds of poems that could be used in short introductions.

Found Poems

The words of a found poem are found in any locale: a newspaper, a sign, the dictionary, a magazine, a story, another poem. Ask students to find a poem by extracting words from an original source and placing them in lines that make at least some kind of sense. (See Chapter 10 , p. 141, for a more elaborate discussion and an example of a found poem.)

Memory Poems

A memory poem is just that: a single memory presented in very spare language. Students might write out a memory as prose, then whittle it down until just the essence of the memory remains. That is the memory poem.

Occasional Poems

As the name implies, occasional poems mark some kind of occasion: a birthday, a wedding, a winning season, an award. An occasional poem might be written *to* someone, on Mother's Day or Father's Day, for example. Whatever the occasion, ask students to try to use concrete language, precise images to convey the occasion for the poem.

Pattern Poems

Pattern poems are written to a preestablished pattern. We suggest you make up some simple patterns, write some class poems to them, then have students make up their own patterns. Approaching this in the form of a game makes it both worthwhile and enjoyable.

Five-Finger Exercises

Although these exercises require the participants to "follow the rules," they also encourage the idea that writing poems can be a form of playing with language. They result in some interesting small poems. You might have students work either individually or in pairs on these poems. (Note: You may want to do some work on the concepts of *abstract* and *concrete* before you begin this exercise.)

The five-finger exercises use the following "givens." Begin by working with the whole class to select the following:

- One abstraction or concept word (examples: *love, friendship, privacy, independence*)
- One color word describing the abstraction (ask: "What color is love, or independence?")
- Three concrete image words that describe the abstraction (ask: "If 'happiness is a warm puppy,' what is friendship, or fear, or anger?")

The stanza pattern (number of lines and words per line) for each of the five poems is on the left. On the right are directions about including certain of the "givens." Poets may include the required words any place in the stanza.

Poem 1: Five lines
    Line 1: Three words   Introduce abstraction and metaphor.
    Line 2: Two words
    Line 3: Four words
    Line 4: One word
    Line 5: Five words

Poem 2: Five lines
    Line 1: Five words   Use color word and at least one of
    Line 2: Three words the concrete image words.
    Line 3: Five words
    Line 4: Three words
    Line 5: Five words

Poem 3: Three lines
    Line 1: Three words This is the Fulcrum Poem: Each word
    Line 2: Three words must have only one syllable.
    Line 3: Three words Use color and abstraction.

Poem 4: One line with five words   Alliteration Poem: All
    words should begin with
    the same consonant sound.
    Use one concrete image
    word in the line.

Poem 5: Six lines   Take a word for a walk. Choose your
    own magic word. Move this word
    through the poem so that it appears
    in each "X" position progressively.
    Use color, abstraction, and concrete
    image words.

```
  X   ____ ____ ____ ____ ____
____   X   ____ ____ ____ ____
____ ____   X   ____ ____ ____
____ ____ ____   X   ____ ____
____ ____ ____ ____   X   ____
____ ____ ____ ____ ____   X
```

After students have finished their poems, have them give one title to the whole set. They may want to title or number each poem separately, as well. Post the poems and have them share with other class members. (Note: The Five-Finger Exercises appear in the *Daybook of Critical Reading and Writing, Grade 9*, pp. 96–97, along with sample student poems.)

Poems in Response to Paintings: "Landscape with the Fall of Icarus"

The relationship between poetry and painting has a long history. Many teachers have built on this tie by having students write poems that are inspired by paintings or that are, in some way, parallel works. One of the most powerful of the paintings that have inspired poems is Pieter Brueghel's "Landscape with the Fall of Icarus." The most famous poem making use of this painting is W. H. Auden's "Musée des Beaux Arts," but there are many others: "Landscape with the Fall of Icarus," by William Carlos Williams; "Lines on Brueghel's 'Icarus,'" by Michael Hamburger; "Icarus," by Lyman Andrews: "To a Friend Whose Work Has Come to Triumph," by Anne Sexton; and "Icarus," by Edward Field..

The myth of Daedalus and Icarus is embedded in our literature and has been explored many times. One of the richest treatments is available at Donna Reiss's Web site: Under the title "Allusion, Artistry, and the Fall of Icarus," Reiss incorporates many poems, paintings, and interactive suggestions for study and for writing. It is well worth looking at.

Specific Icarus Poem Assignment

A very productive suggestion for having students write to the Icarus theme is to have them write as many completions as they can to these two words:

> Flying . . .
> > Falling . . .

Then ask them to compose two stanzas incorporating as many of the phrases in their lists as they want:

> The first begins
> > I am falling . . .
> The second begins
> > I am flying . . .

A variation is to have them write alternative lines, keeping the poem going as long as they can.

After completing this preliminary warmup, followed by a study of the painting and some of the Icarus poems, many students will go on to write their own Icarus poems, as one of my students did:

Icarus

Icarus, come with me.
I feel small wings
growing from my womb.
Let us walk beside the sea.
Let us taste the flesh
of freshly fallen seabirds.
Let us feel the tender oils
of Grecian mermaids.
Icarus, come with me.
The sun will never touch us
with its too many fingers
of light.
We can watch the moon
with its silent albino ponies.
Icarus, I want you
to travel with me forever.
I want you to come
and walk beside metal barges
that have eroded into the tide.
I want to comb your tired feathers.
Let me brush your solemn wings.
Icarus, come with me,
come with me.

My child has fallen.
His wings have melted
into summer clouds.
His eyes have grown soft
from looking at the sun too long.
His once-beautiful blonde feathers
have grown dark and dull.
Icarus, why did you try
to make love with the sun,
with its evil chariot,
with its mirrored beauty.
You should have come with me, Icarus,
I loved you.

Bill Whiteman

III. Writing Poems Using Established Poetic Forms

When we want students to understand poetic forms, we follow the same principles we used with other genres: we have students

- read a number of poems written in a particular form,
- elicit what seem to be the rules of that kind of poem, and then
- attempt to follow those rules to write a poem in that form.

Here are suggestions for writing the haiku, the sonnet, the villanelle, and the sestina.

The Haiku

The haiku, a tightly condensed, three-line Japanese poetic form, is valuable for teaching the use of precise language and concrete image. The challenge is in having students see connections between two statements without making that connection explicit.

Process: For a class experiment with writing a haiku, select two base images, either by having students volunteer them or just selecting them yourself. We find that images from the natural world work particularly well, so we will use *pigeon* and *peacock*.

Working first with the whole class to demonstrate the process, we begin by asking for a sentence that makes a statement about the *pigeon*. Length of line is not important. Sample sentence for the pigeon:

Pigeons cover the ground around the statue.

Then we ask for a sentence for the second image, the peacock:

Peacocks are noisy birds even though they are very beautiful.

At this point, we introduce the form of the haiku: three lines, with five, seven, five syllables.

As a class, working on the overhead or at the board, we begin to work to restructure our images into that form. There is no need to hold to the first images; we let the content evolve from working with form. (Remember Wordsworth's comment that the "matter is in the manner.")

Evolution of the haiku, working on an overhead with students counting syllables (on left) and calling out changes:

Step 1
11   *Pigeons cover the ground around the statue.*
16   *Peacocks are noisy birds even though they are very beautiful.*

Step 2
7   Pigeons cover the statue.
7   Noisy peacocks live in parks.
9   Visitors see the peacocks not the pigeons.

Step 3
6   If pigeons had feathers
4   like the peacock,
5   we would stop and stare.

Final step, a completed class haiku
5   If pigeons only
7   had feathers like the peacock,
5   how we would wonder.

After finishing a class haiku, we suggest beginning a second one, working through a few steps, then leaving it unfinished for each student (or pair) to complete. Finally, students will write their own haiku using images that are important to them.

The Sonnet

The sonnet is often taught in English classes, but rarely written. Many students, if they have heard of the form at all, think of the sonnet as a difficult, obscure kind of poem. They may not realize that contemporary poets are still writing sonnets. Today's poets feel free about taking liberties with the established forms of the sonnet, but most contemporary sonnets still have fourteen lines.

We suggest using *emulation* as a way into having students study sonnets of any era, from Shakespeare to Billy Collins. Give students a sonnet without any mention of what type of poem it is. You might begin with Shakespeare's Sonnet 116, remembering to avoid using the term *sonnet* for now; for more contemporary sonnets, consult an anthology or go to the Web site Sonnets Central at www.sonnets.org. Whatever poem you select, have copies made, preferably in a large font with three spaces between lines. You can, alternatively, have students copy the poem in ink, leaving two spaces between lines, then work on the emulation in pencil.

First, read the poem with the students.

#116

Let me not to the marriage of true minds
Admit impediments. Love is not love
Which alters when it alteration finds,
Or bends with the remover to remove.
O no, it is an ever fixed mark
That looks on tempests and is never shaken;
It is the star to every wand'ring barque,
Whose worth's unknown although his height be taken.

Love's not time's fool, though rosy lips and cheeks
Within his bending sickle's compass come;
Love alters not with his brief hours and weeks,
But bears it out even to the edge of doom.
If this be error and upon me proved,
I never writ, nor no man ever loved.

William Shakespeare

As with any poem that becomes the subject for study, we suggest you spend some time in discussion eliciting ideas from students: have them focus on phrases they like, words they need to clarify, ideas they have about the meaning of the poem. Then have them follow the guidelines for *emulation* (see Chapter 9, "Learning Writing Strategies through Modeling," partly repeated here):

Key Directions for an Emulation:

- Direct students to replace almost every word of the original with a word of their own that serves the same purpose.

- They can repeat such words as *and, but,* and *or*. Prepositions may be kept or replaced; and any form of the verb *to be* may be retained.

- The important thing in doing an emulation is to select a subject that is different from that of the original and stay with it. Note the difference between replacing words with synonyms and words that function the same way in the sentence.

Note: If you are working with students whose first language is not English, you may want them to use synonyms and the same subject. This can be a valuable vocabulary exercise.

We like to have students work in pairs to write their emulations; for most students, it is less tedious and more creative. For this process, you might tell students that they can ignore the rhyme scheme if they want although some may want to try it.

The emulation process takes time and can be frustrating as students work with unfamiliar sentence patterns. This grappling with sentence and poetic form is the purpose of the assignment, however, so help students when they hit blocks and encourage them when they make progress.

After students have finished writing their emulations, have them analyze what they have read and written; at this point, have them count the lines of the Shakespeare poem, look at line length, notice rhyme schemes, and so forth. Now is the time to name the type of poem (if no one in the class has named it) and tell them they have all written poems at least approaching sonnets. It is much easier after this exercise to work with other sonnets in class.

The Villanelle

In this exercise, we suggest that you "back into" the form. Begin with a well-known villanelle: three possibilities readily available in anthologies are Dylan Thomas's "Do Not Go Gentle into That Good Night"; Theodore Roethke's "The Waking"; and Edwin Arlington Robinson's "The House on the Hill." A very long list of villanelles is readily available on the Internet. These poems can often be copied and used for educational purposes.

Read the selected poem or poems aloud, then do what you prefer with the first reading response to a poem. You might have students write a journal response, use some reading response questions, or use Louise Rosenblatt's "What do you make of it?" question. Whatever you do, give students time to think about the poem before looking at its form.

- Have students work in pairs as they look at the number of lines, the meter, the rhyme scheme. When they have finished, ask one group to put their results on the board. If there are variations among the results, discuss them and arrive at what they think might be a description of the form of this poem.
- At that time, name the form, villanelle.

It is much easier to see the pattern of the villanelle by looking at an example and marking the rhyme scheme at the end of each line. We suggest having students go through the poem checking that their analysis fits the traditional pattern.

The traditional villanelle has nineteen lines:

- The lines are grouped into five three-line stanzas (tercets) of any length and a concluding quatrain.
- The villanelle has two end rhymes.
  - The rhyme scheme is *aba,* with the same end-rhyme for the first and last line of each tercet.
  - The rhyme scheme of the end quatrain is *abaa.*
- Two of the lines are repeated:
  - The first line of the first stanza is repeated as the last line of the second and the fourth stanzas, and as the second-to-last line in the concluding quatrain.
  - The third line of the first stanza is repeated as the last line of the third and the fifth stanzas, and as the last line in the concluding quatrain.
- Thus the pattern of line-repetition is as follows:

> A1 b A2 - Lines in first tercet.
> a b A1 - Lines in second tercet.
> a b A2 - Lines in third tercet.
> a b A1 - Lines in fourth tercet.
> a b A2 - Lines in fifth tercet.
> a b A1 A2 - Lines in final quatrain.

- ◆ The lines of the first tercet are represented by "A1 b A2," because the first and third lines rhyme and will be repeated later in the poem.
- ◆ The first line of each subsequent stanzas is shown as "a" because it rhymes with those two lines.
- ◆ The second line ("b") is not repeated but the second line of each subsequent stanza rhymes with that line.

For their own composition, have students either emulate the villanelle they analyzed, find another villanelle and emulate it, or work directly from the description of form that is now on the board or chart paper.

The Sestina

More complex than the villanelle, this form presents an interesting game-like activity for a whole class. That way no one student has to bear the burden of composing this lengthy form.

As with the other forms, we suggest presenting students with one or more sestinas. Again, there are many available on the Internet that can be downloaded for educational purposes. We recommend "Sestina" by Elizabeth Bishop, which can be found on the Web site www.poetry connection.net/poets/Elizabeth_Bishop/2957.

First, have students read and discuss the Bishop poem, then analyze its form, looking for the pattern of repeated words. Put the pattern on the board or overhead.

In a traditional sestina:

- The lines are grouped into six sestets and a concluding tercet. Thus a sestina has thirty-nine lines.
- Lines may be of any length. Their length is usually consistent in a single poem.
- The six words that end each of the lines of the first stanza are repeated in a different order at the end of lines in each of the subsequent five stanzas.
- The repeated words are unrhymed.
- The first line of each sestet after the first ends with the same word as the one that ended the last line of the sestet before it.

- In the closing tercet, each of the six words is used, with one in the middle of each line and one at the end.

- The pattern of word-repetition is as follows, where the words that end the lines of the first sestet are represented by the numbers "1 2 3 4 5 6":

  Group 1, Stanza 1:   1, 2, 3, 4, 5, 6

  Group 2, Stanza 2:   6, 1, 5, 2, 4, 3

  Group 3, Stanza 3:   3, 6, 4, 1, 2, 5

  Group 4, Stanza 4:   5, 3, 2, 6, 1, 4

  Group 5, Stanza 5:   4, 5, 1, 3, 6, 2

  Group 6, Stanza 6:   2, 4, 6, 5, 3, 1

  Teacher Stanza 7, the tercet, has three lines:

  Line one uses words 5 and 2

  Line two uses words 1 and 4

  Line three uses words 3 and 6

Procedure for Writing a Class Sestina: With the whole class contributing, select six words. These words will appear at the ends of lines in each stanza. We suggest referring to the five-finger exercises, not to repeat the words selected for those poems, but to see the range you might use for the sestina. You might, for instance, ask students for six end words such as these:

- an abstraction   (word 1)
- a concrete image   (word 2)
- a color word   (word 3)
- a concrete image   (word 4)
- an animal   (word 5)
- a concrete image   (word 6)

The pattern: You will need six groups, one to write each stanza, 1 through 6. You will write the final tercet.

You might have students use tetrameter, a four-beat line, unless you would rather have them experiment with pentameter, preparatory to reading Shakespeare, for instance.

Have students work in groups to write their stanzas, using the scheme for their ending words. They should try to make some kind of sense, even if it is silly sense, of their stanzas. The shock, of course, comes from having the class hear the entire poem aloud. Because of the repetition of words, there will be an overall kind of sense to the poem. It is both challenging and creative as a poetic activity, even if they will never read or write another sestina in their lives.

IV. Prose Poems

Stein's question, posed at the beginning of this chapter, "What is poetry and if you know what poetry is what is prose," is worth a second look. The concept of prose poetry is certainly not a new one, having had practitioners throughout literary history, but it is enjoying a renaissance. There are many references to prose poetry on the Internet, although only a few prose poems make it into school anthologies. While it is a popular medium with students, we prefer to introduce it after students already have an idea of the elements that we look for in poetry: imagery, metaphor, condensed language, precise diction—all characteristics of prose poetry, too, but with less attention to form.

A succinct definition of prose poetry, from Peggy Prater, is "poetry written as prose; in other words, it is a hybrid form combining poetry and prose. The prose poem has all of the essential elements of traditional poetry written in verse. It has rhythm, rhyme, repetition, assonance, consonance, and imagery." Janet Lowenbach, in an interview regarding her prose poem in *Double Room,* a journal of prose poetry and flash fiction, responds to the question of what prose poetry is with this statement: "My piece is both a prose poem and flash fiction. Why must we choose when the two forms have nourished this emerging mode of expression and given birth to a new way of seeing truth that is both poetry and image, rhythm and condensed meaning wound round and round like a chrysalis and not revealed until you penetrate both the writer's intent and your own experience? Prose poems expose life because they delve beneath the surface into the borderless things. They are images made, scattered about the page but merging through rhythm, mood, color, into the characters of a new idiom."

One prose poet that students will probably have read is Walt Whitman. We suggest having them read some pages from *Leaves of Grass,* then writing their own version of a prose poem on any topic of their choosing. (The entire *Leaves of Grass* is available online; just search by that title and you can download any of the sections.) You might begin with one of the following passages (the second one is used earlier in the section on parapoetics):

> **1.**
>
> I celebrate myself, and sing myself,
> And what I assume you shall assume,
> For every atom belonging to me as good belongs to you.
>
> I loafe and invite my soul,
> I lean and loafe at my ease observing a spear of summer grass.

My tongue, every atom of my blood, form'd from this soil, this
   air,
Born here of parents born here from parents the same, and their
   parents the same,
I, now thirty-seven years old in perfect health begin,
Hoping to cease not till death.

Creeds and schools in abeyance,
Retiring back a while sufficed at what they are, but never
   forgotten,
I harbor for good or bad, I permit to speak at every hazard,
Nature without check with original energy.

2.

I hear America singing, the varied carols I hear,
Those of mechanics, each one singing his as it should be blithe
   and strong,
The carpenter singing his as he measures his plank or beam,
The mason singing his as he makes ready for work, or leaves
   off work,
The boatman singing what belongs to him in his boat, the
   deckhand singing on the steamboat deck,
The shoemaker singing as he sits on his bench, the hatter
   singing as he stands,
The wood-cutter's song, the ploughboy's on his way in the
   morning, or at the noon intermission or at sundown,
The delicious singing of the mother, or of the young wife at
   work, or of the girl sewing or washing,
Each singing what belongs to him or her and to none else,
The day what belongs to the day - at night the party of young
   fellows, robust, friendly,
Singing with open mouths their strong melodious songs.

In writing their own prose poems, you might suggest that they begin
with a line from Whitman; this practice will often be enough to get them
started if they need an external starter.

Assessing Student Poems

Teachers desiring to construct a rubric for assessing student poetry (or
poems by published poets, for that matter) might consider the following:

- What was the intent of the writer with regard to
   - purpose?
   - audience?
   - form?
- How well did the writer accomplish his or her intent? (The fol-

lowing questions are examples of the kinds of questions that
might fit a particular writing assignment.)

- ◆ If the intent was to convey a personal experience, how did
  the language of the poem succeed in doing that?
- ◆ If the intent was to conduct a different purpose, like making a political statement, how did the language of the poem
  succeed in doing that?
- ◆ If the intent was to write a haiku or a sonnet or other fixed
  form, how does the final poem measure up?

- ■ How effectively does the writer use such poetic resources as
  imagery, metaphor, symbol, paradox, irony, allusion, sound
  repetition, rhythm, and pattern?

We suggest having students grapple with these questions, and others
they might think of, and, working in groups, come up with a rubric
which they can use to assess their poems.

The Portfolio: We strongly advocate the use of a portfolio of poems for assessment; by looking at an entire booklet of poems, you can
see how well students achieved their purposes (and yours!) in their
poems. A critical component of any portfolio collection is the student's
reflections about the contents. The reflective piece should, in essence,
be a commentary on the student's experiences in writing the poems and
contain, as well, a self-assessment of the poems, using the rubric the class
designed.

To Close: A Naming of Parts

To close the poetry section, we offer you Adrianne Marcus's poem about
teaching, a play on Henry Reed's "Naming of Parts." Most of us have
vivid memories of the coach/administrator using martial metaphors at
the first assembly as we entered into another school year. Unfortunately,
it seems more apt now than ever, decry it as we will.

> **Teaching: Rules of Engagement**
>
> First, learn their names. You cannot command
> troops unless you know their names, their ranks.
> Now, give the simplest orders first. Today
> we will have the naming of parts, noun, pro-
> noun, anti-noun. Tomorrow, verbs.
>
> Sophia, the dark haired girl in the second row
> looks puzzled. She is twisting her hair into knots
> chewing on her pencil. You must tell her, gently,
> Erasers do not make a good lunch.
> Brittany, the blonde warrior, fidgets, wants

to get on with this class action, get outside,
head to cheerleading practice. Now,
show them a poem. Explain that the words
are peripheral, that style comes before substance,
and if you have to choose, go with style.

They will understand that. Cropped tops,
low rider jeans. See if they can make a poem
out of fabric. Whole cloth. Let them take
out their rage against parents and teachers,
incomplete sentences, misspellings

in double time. Try to be patient.
In six weeks they will complete basic
training and then you can go on to
complex sentences. Perhaps a Sestina.
They will learn to appreciate form.

They'll be combat ready.

Adrianne Marcus

Note

1. Poets through the ages have attempted to define poetry: Samuel Taylor Coleridge exemplifies the difficulties in this passage from his *Biographia Literaria:* "Poetry is the work of the imagination, that power which reveals itself in the balance or reconciliation of the opposite or discordant qualities: of sameness, with difference; of the general, with the concrete; the idea, with the image; the individual, with the representative; the sense of novelty and freshness, with old and familiar objects; a more than usual state of emotion, with more than usual order; judgment ever awake and steady self possession, with enthusiasm and feeling profound or vehement; and while it blends and harmonizes the natural and the artificial, still subordinates art to nature; the manner to the matter, and our admiration of the poet to our sympathy with the poetry."

9 Learning Writing Strategies through Modeling

What is imitated is not merely form or structure but grammatical and rhetorical principles that underlie the structure of the model.

Frank J. D'Angelo

I. The Place of Modeling in Teaching Writing

While modeling is widely used as a way of helping students learn to read closely, we will focus in this chapter on using the natural inclination to model what one is reading primarily to extend the range of possibilities in one's own writing. The overriding goal, however, is to help students become both transactive, discerning readers and inventive, perceptive writers.

Modeling works well with students of all ability levels, whether homogeneously or heterogeneously grouped. It is especially effective in working with second-language students. My own classroom experience, as well as testimony from writers and researchers, indicates that modeling, which includes various permutations of imitations and derivations, closely emulates the natural stages we go through in the acquisition of language. Many writers have talked about how, during their formative years, they either consciously or subconsciously imitated the styles of writers whom they admired. In this chapter, we will focus on making the processes of thinking and learning explicit for students, urging them to explore their own ways of making sense not only of what they read but in what they write.

All students will, through modeling practices, produce writing that incorporates the stylistic and literary elements of poems, stories, and essays they have studied. The literary pieces students write will demonstrate many of the following characteristics: They may

- use specific literary devices with awareness and appropriateness (e.g., imagery, metaphor, symbol, irony, personification)
- use stylistic devices characteristic of the authors they have studied

- use structural modeling to show awareness of the organization of works they have studied
- show evidence of choices about form
- use language effectively, showing an awareness of choice of diction to achieve specific intents
- use a variety of sentence structures to achieve a particular style

Research Support for Modeling

One of the three research articles included in the May 1994 issue of *Research in the Teaching of English* is "Prose Modeling and Metacognition: The Effect of Modeling on Developing a Metacognitive Stance toward Writing," by Elizabeth A. Stolarek from Ferris State University. In this extensive research project, Stolarek explores the effectiveness of using prose modeling in the composition classroom. The results of the study "indicate that novice writers who are given a model of an unfamiliar prose form to imitate respond in a manner which is more introspective and evaluative and far more similar to the responses of expert writers than do novice writers who are not given a model" (154).

Theorists who support modeling, according to Stolarek, "assert that style can be improved through the modification of classical imitation exercises (Corbett, 1965, 1971), that models acquaint students with complicated structural conventions and patterns they have not previously used in their writing, thus enhancing creativity (McCampbell, 1966), or that creative imitation promotes originality in student writing by providing students with stylistic options, thus freeing them to concentrate on invention (D'Angelo, 1973). Others, such as Purves and Purves (1986) consider knowledge of models one of the three forms of knowledge (the others being semantic and pragmatic knowledge) imperative in learning how to write within the context of a particular culture" (154–55).

Stolarek goes on to point out that while Paul Eschholz "introduces models as an intervention technique for individual students who are experiencing difficulties in their writing, thus helping them to achieve a better sense of purpose, form, and direction without stifling creativity" (155), her own study was, she says, "based on the belief that prose modeling can serve an even larger purpose. It explores whether prose modeling can promote an introspective, evaluative, metacognitive stance toward writing both in expert and novice writers" (155).

Integrating Modeling into Classroom Assignments

There are a number of ways that modeling provides support for both reading and writing instruction:

1. As a catalyst for writing, particularly for *reluctant writers*. It immediately provides a structure and takes away much of the threat of the blank page.

2. As an *introduction to poetic forms*. Again, much of the onus is gone when students first model a poem, then discover its form by analyzing their own work as well as the original.

3. To encourage *close reading of a text*. As part of the study of a novel, particularly a difficult one stylistically, we have students choose a representative passage (they must decide what is representative), model it, then do a structural analysis of it. This practice enhances both their understanding of the content of the original (it slows down their reading!) and their grasp of the author's style. Students often work together in pairs or groups on this activity.

4. To teach *awareness of diction and diction analysis*. We ask students to choose a passage and, in pairs or small groups, analyze its tone by exploring the use of diction, detail, and syntax. They might write an analysis of the passage. Either after or before the analysis, they choose a different subject from that of the original and emulate the passage, working consciously to create a particular tone or effect. Students can also write emulations of one another's work, accompanied by an analysis and critique. This last activity is one I usually reserve for students who are already quite proficient in writing.

5. As a way of *teaching English language sentence patterns to second-language learners*. By modeling, students are able to internalize the natural flow of English sentences.

6. As part of an *intensive author study*. Students read a variety of works (short stories, essays, poems, novels, plays) by a single author. They select sections they believe to be representative of the author's style and analyze them from the standpoint of diction, tone, and idea progression. They model a short section. Their final piece in this complex assignment, which also involves some secondary-source research, is to write a full piece in the style of the selected author, showing through their choice of subject matter, genre, syntax, voice, and tone that they have developed and internalized a familiarity with the author's style.

II. Formats for Modeling Instruction

> *We learn to write by reading the poets we love over and over again and asking ourselves two questions: what are they doing and why are they doing it?*
>
> Erica Jong

The following types of modeling move from simple to complex. That does not mean that you need to teach them in this progression or that you need to use all of them. Once you are familiar with some of these approaches, you will undoubtedly see additional possibilities for using modeling in other ways.

> Type 1: Loose Modeling: retain basic form and some starter words
>
> Type 2: Response Modeling: respond to original content; retain tone
>
> Type 3: Emulation: replace original, word-for-word by function
>
> Type 4: Writing by the Rules: follow the form of a piece or a genre
>
> Type 5: Structural Modeling: model the thought progressions of the original
>
> Type 6: The Paralogue: create a parallel dialogue with the author
>
> Type 7: Style Modeling: write a substantial piece in the style of an author

Modeling, Type 1: Loose Modeling

For teaching loose modeling, select a poem or prose passage from the text you are studying or introduce a simple poem specifically for this practice. Many teachers have used William Carlos Williams's poem "This Is Just to Say" for an introduction to loose modeling. Follow the directions below to write a class model. Once you have done a simple practice such as that one, choose a more complex poem and have students work either individually or in pairs to write a loose model.

Directions for Loose Modeling

Have students follow these steps.

- Students underline key words or phrases which they will use in their own poems.
- Students select subject different from the one in the original poem. If the poem is about a person, for example, have them think about a specific person they know well enough to de-

scribe in exact, concrete images. (A *concrete image* is one that presents a picture of something tangible, something that has form and shape.)

- Using the key words from the original, students model the poem. They may write longer or shorter lines, but keep the same number of lines in each stanza and retain the key words they have selected.

- When they have finished, have them give the poem a title that echoes the original.

- Underneath their title, they should sign their versions, then write, "after (poem title) by (poem's author)." This acknowledges their debt but allows them to retain credit for their model.

Modeling, Type 2: Response Modeling

In response modeling, students read an original passage (either from a text you are studying, one they are reading on their own, or a poem or passage selected for the exercise) and write a response to the content, retaining only the general form—prose or poem, dialogue or reflection. The focus in this practice is to try to identify the *tone* of the original and maintain that in the response. You might begin with a short poem, model it with the class, then give them a different passage for them to model. This practice works well with partners as well as individual students.

We have found that response modeling is useful for argumentative writing, too; asking students to respond to an editorial or position piece, retaining the tone of the original but expressing personal opinions, is challenging and interesting to them.

Modeling, Type 3: Emulation

In this practice, select a prose passage or poem by an author who has a definitive style, perhaps the use of an obviously repetitive sentence pattern. Ernest Hemingway provides many possibilities, but you can find examples in the texts you are currently teaching. Students "try on" the style of the selected author by *emulating* or reproducing the pattern exactly, word for word, only using their own words to replace original author's.

Selecting a Passage for the Emulation

In this practice, it is important to select a passage with a style that is just at the upper level of that which students are currently able to produce. For example, if they are consistently writing simple sentences, find a passage that contains some complex (but not too many) sentences. If they overuse prepositional phrases, find a passage that conveys complex ideas without such phrases. If they are writing with too many generalizations, find a passage that is rich with concrete imagery.

Key Directions for an Emulation

Have students follow these steps:

- Direct students to replace almost every word of the original with a word of their own that serves the same purpose. If they are familiar with the names of the parts of speech, that means replace every noun with a noun, verb with a verb, adjective with an adjective, and so on. This rule can be modified, but I generally ask students to replace all nouns, verbs, and modifiers.

- There are places where they can use the words of the original if they want to: words such as *and, but,* and *or;* may be repeated; prepositions (words such as *in, out, above, through,* and *with*) may be used or replaced; and any form of the verb *to be* (*am, is, was, were,* etc.) may be used as in the original.

- Explain to students that the important thing in doing an emulation is to select a subject that is different from that of the original and stay with it. *Clarify the difference between replacing words with synonyms and words that function the same way in the sentence.*

For second language learners or students not proficient in vocabulary, you may wish to make this practice one of finding synonyms rather than words that mean something different but function as do the originals. We suggest using this variation on an individual basis rather than as a class assignment.

Hints

The easiest way to do an emulation is to copy the original on paper, *in ink,* leaving *two* spaces below each line. Write the emulation, *in pencil,* on the line below, keeping the words lined up. These directions might seem like a lot of work for a short exercise, but they will save time and energy in the long run. If you have students writing in a computer lab, they can just vary the font size and color for the emulation.

Don't miss this next step! When they have finished their emulations, tell students to keep on writing for another sentence or more on the extra line allowed, carrying their idea further. *The point of this part of the practice is to continue to write in the style of the original without the support of its sentence pattern.* By taking this extra step, students internalize the structure and make it one of the options they will have as they develop their own styles of writing. Be sure to let students know they may continue to write in this fashion as long as they choose. We have had students find that this practice starts them on a major piece of their own, one in which they use sentence patterns they had not used before.

An Audible Check

Have students read their emulations to partners or small groups and ask whether their listeners noticed when the emulation stopped and their own writing began. The most successful emulations appear to be seamless.

Modeling, Type 4: Writing by the Rules

When we talk about not wanting students to follow formulas in their writing, we are generally talking about providing students with the features of a genre before they understand what the genre is, or giving them steps in writing an essay. We all know the many programs and books that used to advocate having students follow the "thesis, 3 supporting statements, conclusion (restating the thesis)" model. We hope it is clear from our approach to having students read and elicit characteristics of a genre before writing in that mode that we do not support such a practice.

Emulation and Poetic Form

The previous type of modeling, emulation, provides the framework for having students learn and practice various forms of writing from already published works. For this type, we suggest beginning with some simple forms without established names but with rules that students must follow, lending this type especially well to poetry. Make the forms up; have your students make them up. In Chapter 8, "Poetry," the Five-Finger Exercises present an elaborated set of "made-up" forms, a series of game poems that establish simple forms: ask students to model them, then move on to limericks, haiku (simple only in their external form), ballads (bring in song lyrics), and other more complex forms. Some of the more formal kinds of poetry students might emulate—the sonnet, the villanelle, and the sestina—are also presented in Chapter 8.

Modeling, Type 5: Structural Modeling

For this practice, students model the thought progressions of the base text. Select two short essays of about a page each; look for essays that include diverse ways of thinking about a topic, preferably reflective pieces that make some use of metaphoric thinking. Good places to find such essays are in magazines ("Talk of the Town" in *The New Yorker* is a goldmine for this kind of reflective piece). Place one essay on an overhead. Make copies of both essays for each student. You might make a few extra as some are likely to get very messy before students are finished.

Procedure

Part 1.

- Hand out copies of the first essay. This one should be on an overhead and will be used to demonstrate the process.
- Go through the essay line by line, with the students, marking the elements that show the kind of thinking the writer has shown. Mark and label such things as these:
  - ◆ Introduces topic
  - ◆ Uses firsthand knowledge (personal experience)
  - ◆ Uses secondhand knowledge (references to other writers, film, television, etc.)
  - ◆ Makes metaphoric leaps of thought
  - ◆ Digresses from topic
  - ◆ Comes back to main idea
  - ◆ Draws inferences
  - ◆ Speaks directly to the reader
  - ◆ Employs words that are of limited usage, particular to a profession or a sport, for instance
  - ◆ Makes generalizations
  - ◆ Comes to a conclusion
- Have students mark their own copies of this essay.
- Discuss the progression of thought in this essay.

Part 2:

- Hand out copies of the second essay.
- Have students work either individually or in pairs to mark and label all of the kinds of thinking they can find in this essay.
- Have students discuss the way the writer's mind seemed to move through the essay.

Part 3:

- Students work individually on writing their own essays.
- Have them select a topic to write about; it should be one that will involve them in thinking in more than one way about their topic.

- Have students make a plan on a full sheet of paper designating the way the analyzed essay progressed:

Labels showing progression of thought in the analyzed essay	Prewriting: Ideas for each part of the essay I plan to write

- After students have filled out a form such as this one, have them draft their essays.
- Students should meet with their partners to help each other on the specific parts.
- Once their essays are finished, ask them to edit them for correctness before handing them in.

As a final step, ask students to write a short assessment of their work with this assignment. They might deal with such topics as whether it was easy or hard to follow the thinking of the original writer and whether it was hard to emulate the progression of thought.

Modeling, Type 6: The Paralogue

In constructing a paralogue, the writer actually enters into a kind of dialogue with the author. The prefix *para* means alongside or by the side of, and the word root *log* or *logue* means written or spoken language. So a *paralogue* refers to a piece of writing in which a reader responds in a parallel way to the author, either line by line or section by section. The result is a piece of writing in two voices, the original author's and the responding author's.

Selecting a Text for the Paralogue

Use a passage from a text you are studying or select one specifically for this modeling practice. We have found reflective essays or poems to be especially provocative for writing the paralogue. Select a passage or poem that can easily be divided into five or six sections. You might also use a descriptive or reflective passage from a novel. We have found that it is interesting to give students a piece they haven't read before, instruct them not to read ahead, and follow the directions. This procedure allows for a creative unfolding of the paralogue.

(Examples of the process and finished paralogues appear in the *Daybook of Critical Reading and Writing*, grade 10, using a passage from Alan Lightman's *Einstein's Dreams*, and in *Recasting the Text: Inquiry-Based Activities for Comprehending and Composing*, using Barry Lopez's *River Notes*. See Works Cited for bibliographic information.)

Directions for Creating a Paralogue

Instruct students to set up a page in two columns as indicated. They will use this format for the rough draft of the paralogue.

Original Author's Words	Your Words

Directions

1. For this modeling practice, you will read a short passage of text. Read just the first section of the text. You may not know what the author is writing about, but that is OK at this point. Writing the paralogue will let you see that you often can understand the tone or feeling of a piece even when you are not sure of its meaning.

2. To begin the rough draft of your paralogue, select a sentence or phrase from the passage you have just read. You may be drawn to it because of the meaning or just because of the sound or the tone of it. Write this sentence or phrase on the left side of your page, the original author's side.

3. Now, on the right side of the page, your side, write a phrase or sentence of your own, in response to the sentence you wrote on the left.

4. When you have written your sentence, read the next passage from the selected text. Follow the same procedure that you did in steps 2 and 3, selecting a sentence or phrase from the passage, then answering it with a sentence of your own.

5. Now go on to read the next passage.

6. Continue the same pattern: select a sentence from the text, copy it in column 1 of your page, and write your response in column 2. Then read the next passage.

7. When you reach the final section of the passage, make your response sound like a conclusion.

8. To turn your rough draft into a finished paralogue: Read your rough draft now as a whole, from left to right, sentence by sentence. First read the original author's words, then your own, as you would a dialogue. At this point, make any changes you wish. You may go back and add or subtract words from the author's side, but don't use any words or phrases here that are not part of the original. On your side, change anything you like to make it read more smoothly. You will probably be surprised at how much like a dialogue it sounds. When you are satisfied with the words, give your paralogue a title of your own and make a final copy of it, using the following pattern:

Your Title Here

A Paralogue by (original author's name) and (your name)

Original author's words......................

                Your words........................

Original author's words......................

                Your words........................

Original author's words......................

                Your words........................

Original author's words......................

                Your words........................

Original author's words......................

                Your words........................

Reading the Paralogue

The last step, before publishing, is to have students read their paralogues aloud with partners. Have one student read the original author's words, then the writer of the paralogue his or her part. Then they change roles for the partner's paralogue. Once they have read them through a couple of times, you might want to have them read their paralogues for the class.

Modeling, Type 7: Style Modeling

Example: Author Style Study

In preparing to study a single novelist's work, students engage in the following steps (a student may select from the teacher's list or have an individual choice approved, but each student must find at least one other student who will read the same author). (The preliminary steps in this process were first presented in Chapter 3 but continue beyond the suggestions for interpretation in that chapter.)

Directions for Students:

1. Read at least three of the author's novels, keeping a double-entry journal during the reading.

2. Get together with the other people in the class who have read this author for their study.

3. After discussion of the works read, focus on dominant themes, ideas, symbols, kinds of characters, typical settings, etc., common to this author's work.

4. Prepare a group graphic display dealing with whatever your group feels is most significant about this author's work. The graphic may include both visual and verbal ingredients.

5. Using the graphic and whatever other ideas the group has, present your author to the class. (Some groups may design author interviews, dramatize scenes, portion out sections for separate student presentations, etc.) Follow the presentation with class discussion.

6. At this point in the author study project, each student writes an interpretive essay on some aspect of the author's work.

7. Optional: After students have read a novel and seen a film based on that novel, ask groups to compare the two works with regard to plot and character motivation. After discussion of the various findings of different groups, ask students to write an interpretive essay on some aspect of the work that they found treated differently in the two media. (Examples of readily available film/novel combinations include *Lord of the Flies, To Kill a Mockingbird, Cannery Row, East of Eden, Great Expectations,* and *A Separate Peace.*)

The following aspect of the project, a study of the author's style, augments the description of the author study in Chapter 3. After students have read the three novels by their selected author, they engage in a study of the author's style. For this study, have students follow the following guidelines:

Directions:

1. Select a passage that you think sounds most like the author's voice or style. It should be at least a substantial paragraph. Try to find a passage that you would recognize as that writer's work wherever you found it.

2. Analyze that passage to discover all you can about how it is written. Look for (and make notes about) these things:

   a. Sentence length

   b. Sentence complexity

   c. Word choice: Are there any unusual words? Mostly simple words? Words with obscure meanings?

   d. Verb patterns: Mostly active voice? Mostly passive voice? Many "to be" words?

   e. Subject matter: Is the subject one that you have found typical of this writer?

   f. Sentence patterns: Are there a lot of introductory adverbial clauses? A lot of prepositional phrases? Any unusual sentence patterns?

   g. Any other elements of style that you found in this passage?

3. Write a careful emulation of that passage. See Modeling Type 2, Emulation, for directions.

4. Be sure to continue the emulation for a few sentences beyond the original.

5. Write a short explanation of the author's style, using your emulation to support your ideas about what makes it "sound" like your selected writer.

As a final, optional piece, we like to have our students write a short story in the style of their selected author. This is a major assignment, one that profits from the student groups that have formed during the author study. This assignment shows very clearly whether the student has internalized the style of the author and been able to incorporate the author's stylistic patterns into a new piece. Students find this assignment challenging and intellectually stimulating. Most of them are very proud of "their" stories.

III. A Little Metacognition on Modeling

At some point in the class, after students have experienced two or three kinds of modeling, take some time to have them think about what they have learned about how they work, how they think, and, of course, how they read and write. Modeling is a process that requires close reading, often with careful attention to the way words are put together, which is another way of looking at grammar. It helps them understand tone and feeling by having them create the same tone and feeling in their models as occur in the originals.

Modeling is a way of studying structure without analyzing it, by imitating it. Most of all, modeling allows students to experience different authors' ways of composing. When they have finished a model, they know a lot about the author who wrote the original and they have internalized options that they can now use in their own writing.

10 Teaching Grammar in Contexts *for* Writing

Louann Reid

I take the rules of grammar
*   and guides to good language*
and clutch them
*   to heart-and-mind.*

> *The Art of Writing: Lu Chi's Wen Fu*

Scenario: A Typical Lament

Alice, a graduate of our master's program in English education, teaches in a local junior high school. In a recent meeting to explore better alignment between the university's teacher preparation curriculum and the school district's literacy curriculum, she lamented, "I know I'm not supposed to teach grammar in isolation, but the parents and administrators expect me to teach it. The state test requires that students identify parts of speech and select the 'correct' editing of sentences. The linguistics courses I took were good, but they don't help me teach eighth graders to identify nouns, verbs, and dangling participles. I don't want to use drills and exercises from the district-approved workbook, so I try to teach minilessons from the students' writing, but I just don't see any improvement. Their writing is still full of misspellings, they can't use apostrophes, and if I have to correct *their, there*, and *they're* again I'm going to scream. What am I supposed to do about grammar?"

Alice is not alone in her frustration. Wherever English teachers gather, conversations about writing repeatedly include some variation of "What am I supposed to do about grammar?" Her remarks reveal important elements of the ongoing discussions about teaching grammar:

- the word *grammar* used to encompass language structure (parts of speech), conventions (apostrophes), and usage (choosing among their/there/they're)
- an assumption that writing will improve if grammar is taught
- a belief that students will be more interested in contextualized minilessons than in decontextualized drills

Alice clearly recognizes the imperatives to teach grammar—high-stakes testing and community expectations—and she wants to do what's best for the students. Over the years, such discussions—held in our conventions, journals, and teachers' lounges—have ranged along a continuum from rancorous to enlightening. But Alice still needs to know what to do to help her students write papers that are interesting and technically skillful, the two working criteria that Dan Kirby, Dawn Latta Kirby, and Tom Liner offer.

While Constance Weaver and others such as Rei Noguchi have offered ways to teach grammar in the context *of* writing, I think we need to go beyond their suggestions. Teaching grammar in contexts *for* writing means recognizing the centrality of language in the English language arts and using language as a bridge between the complementary processes of comprehending and composing. We need to help students understand the resources available to them as they use language to construct and communicate knowledge, information, and ideas effectively. We can start by teaching grammar in the contexts of reading and writing.

Value of Context in Teaching and Learning

The question, though, remains: What practices *are* effective in helping students understand language structures in ways that have an impact on their writing? Weaver makes a strong case for teaching grammar in the context of writing and Nancie Atwell's approach to instruction through minilessons in reading and writing workshops is another contextualized practice.

What I want to argue is that we need to pay greater attention to reading as a context for teaching grammar. We need not abandon successful practices that teach grammar in the context of writing, of course, but such contextualization is not completely satisfactory. Recall Alice's complaint: no matter how many minilessons she does, student writing does not seem to improve.

Reading as a Context for Teaching Grammar

Reading as a context for grammar instruction that will affect writing in a positive way makes sense for a number of reasons.

- The processes for constructing meaning in reading and writing are similar. According to Robert Tierney and David Pearson, "Both are acts of composing. From a reader's perspective, meaning is created as a reader uses his background of experience together with the author's cues to come to grips both with what the writer is getting him to do or think *and* what the reader decides and creates for himself. As a writer writes, she uses her own background of experience to generate ideas and, in order to produce a text which is considerate to her idealized reader, filters these drafts through her judgments about what her reader's background of experience will be, what she wants to say, and what she wants to get the reader to think or do" (568).

- The processes used for reading are compatible with processes for learning language structure and use—close attention, prediction based on language clues, constructing meaning, building concepts, and so forth.
- The bridge between comprehending and composing is language. Through language we make sense of the world and we communicate with others (Britton, Donaldson).

What would it look like to teach language structure and use in the context of reading? The four activities that follow can be used in their current form with most middle school and secondary school students, but they could also be made more or less challenging by changing the texts used.

Activities

The activities have two characteristics in common. *First, they call on the three Cs of motivation—choice, community, and curiosity.* Students want to learn when they engage in activities that do not have just one answer, that require divergent thinking. Working with friends is often motivating, so the activities include an element of co-construction or sharing. And students are motivated to continue when their curiosity is piqued, when they have a purpose for inquiry.

The activities also integrate the language arts, calling on students to read, write, speak, and listen. In a semester or yearlong class, other activities would need to be devised that ask students to use their multiple intelligences or to construct and communicate knowledge through viewing and visually representing it. This integration of the language arts is also beneficial to English language learners who are acquiring academic English. MaryCarmen Cruz offers several classroom-tested strategies in "Can English Language Learners Acquire Academic English?"

Teachers could use these activities at various stages in students' reading. "Combining Sentences; Exploring Effects" (Activity 1) could be used before reading a book as a way to provide students with material for predictions about content. Or it could be used to help students understand sentence construction during and after reading. Activities to help students understand an author's style or decisions about language resources (Activities 1, 2, and 3) could best be used after reading. Sequence for the fourth activity depends on the language phenomenon targeted. The activity on apostrophes would come only after much reading and discussion of other aspects of the text.

It is important that students first read for pleasure and comprehension, unless the activity is used for prediction or setting a purpose for reading. Just as editing often comes at a later stage in writing, so should explicit awareness of language in reading. In fact, it may be useful to think of stages of construction of meaning from reading that parallel stages of constructing meaning for writing. Tierney and Pearson did that in some detail in "Toward a Composing Model of Reading." The "Reading-writing connection" in each activity draws from their model.

The benchmarks in the following activities are drawn from the Colorado Model Content Standards for Reading and Writing, which are similar to many state documents that specify what students will know and be able to do. As part of adapting the activities for your own students, you would also adjust them to meet your state's or district's expectations.

I. Combining Sentences, Exploring Effects

Central concept: By combining kernel sentences in various ways and discussing the effects of those combinations, students can make decisions about writing their own sentences.

Reading-writing connection: Readers and writers set a purpose, call on background knowledge, and create questions in the planning stage, which is how the activity is written. If this activity is used for style analysis, it would fit in the revision stage, when readers and writers reexamine the meaning they have constructed.

Benchmarks: using simple, compound, complex, and compound-complex sentences in writing and speaking; using phrases and clauses for purposes of modification and parallel structure in writing and speaking (10).

Assignment for Students

Read the kernel sentences that follow. They are taken from Victor Martinez's *Parrot in the Oven: Mi Vida*, which you will begin reading tomorrow. Notice that spaces separate groups of sentences. Your task is to combine all of the kernel sentences in one group into one or more well-written sentences. Write your sentences on another sheet of paper or in the white space to the right of the text.

After you have created all of the combined sentences, compare yours with those of two or three other students in a small group. Make notes about the differences in your results. Why do you like some combinations better than others?

Next, compare your sentences to the ones Martinez wrote. Which sentences are more effective and why? Which ones do you like better?

Note to teacher: If you have students repeat this activity with several sentences from the book, you could ask them to use those to predict what the book will be about.

> Nardo was a dark clump.
> Nardo was beside me.
> Nardo was on the bed.
>
> I whispered to him.
> There was no answer.
>
> His face could barely be seen.
> His face was in the murky darkness.
>
> I wondered.
> My wondering was whether I should wake him.
> I was about to touch his shoulder.
> He snatched.
> His snatching was at the blanket.
> He tucked himself.
> His tucking was into a cocoon.
>
> I saw a shadow.
> The shadow flickered.
> It was under the door.
> I slipped.
> My slipping was out of bed.

From *Parrot in the Oven: Mi Vida*, by Victor Martinez (New York: Harper, 1996):

> Beside me, Nardo was a dark clump on the bed. I whispered to him, but there was no answer. His face could barely be seen in the murky darkness. I wondered whether I should wake him, but just as I was about to touch his shoulder, he snatched at the blanket and tucked himself into a cocoon. I saw a shadow flicker under the door and slipped out of bed. (152)

II. Using Phrases and Clauses

Central concept: Understanding ways in which phrases and clauses can be used as modifiers helps students create syntactically more mature text.

Reading-writing connection: revision.

Benchmark: "[using] phrases and clauses for purposes of modification [. . .] in writing and speaking" (Colorado 17).

Assignment for Students

A "found poem" is a poem composed entirely of words selected from another text, such as one you are reading for a literature circle or whole-class discussion. (See Chapter 8, p. 107, for a brief discussion of found poetry.) The purpose of writing a found poem for this assignment is to add to your insights about the novel by looking at part of it in a different way—the compressed expression of poetry. Participial phrases, which are groups of words beginning with a past or present participle, function as adjectives and can be highly effective modifiers. In your found poem, emphasize participial phrases, although you may also include clauses. If you need more information about participles, phrases, and clauses, consult a writing handbook or ask your teacher.

Steps for creating a found poem:

1. Decide on a topic that interests you, such as a particular setting, person, or event in the novel. You may also choose to have your found poem convey an important aspect of the novel.

2. Skim through the novel to find as many relevant clauses and participial phrases as you can. Flag them with sticky notes or write them down on another piece of paper, being sure to note the page numbers so you can find them again. You may select phrases from any part of the novel and, if necessary, you may modify the form of a word and/or add small words. However, try not to change the text much; you need to leave it as you "found" it.

3. Arrange the phrases and clauses to create a poem that represents the novel yet presents it in a new way.

The following sample is from Chapters 1 through 4 of *Bless the Beasts and Children,* by Glendon Swarthout (New York: Pocket, 1970/1995), a novel about a group of boys that others view as misfits who are together at a summer camp near a buffalo ranch:

From Boys to Men

A brood of cabins,
Nested in the ponderosa,
Feathered by the trees.

A range of mountains,
A herd of huge black beasts,
Snorting clouds and bumping heaven
With its humps.

Cotton, Teft, Shecker, Goodenow,
Lally One and Two,
Some men with guns,
Going somewhere,
To do something dangerous.

III. Misplacing Modifiers

Central concept: When students read from the writer's perspective, they can better understand the craft of the piece. Examining the effects of diction and questioning the author's decisions encourage students to read as writers.

Reading-writing connection: revising.

Benchmark: "[using] modifiers [. . .] in writing and speaking" (Colorado 16).

Note: This will be more effective if students see each part of the assignment as they are to complete it rather than all at once.

Assignment for Students

1. Most of the modifiers in the following paragraph have been removed. Read the paragraph to form an initial impression.

Although we moved, the house held my memories, my fears and questions. It was a matchbox. Next to it stood a garage. The weather battered it. The backyard was a jungle. Vegetation appeared to grow down. There were trees, weeds, foxtails and grass. A tree grew and roots covered every bit of ground, while branches scraped the windows. A sway filled the bit.

What is your initial impression of this place? Jot down a few words or sketch your impression in the box.

2. The following adjectives and adverbs (either single words or phrases) were removed from the paragraph. Quickly skim over them to form an impression. In a pen or pencil of a different color, add to your initial impression in the box above.

> around the Watts area
>
> on 105th Street
>
> near McKinley Avenue
>
> earliest
>
> earliest
>
> small
>
> of a place
>
> tiny
>
> with holes through the walls and an unpainted barnlike quality
>
> into a leaning shed
>
> from the sky
>
> banana
>
> huge
>
> "sperm"
>
> (named that because they stank like semen when you cut them)
>
> yellowed
>
> avocado
>
> in the middle of the yard
>
> tearing up cement walks
>
> bedroom
>
> of clothes
>
> on some lines
>
> little
>
> of grassy area
>
> its
>
> just behind the house
>
> its

3. Now, use your understanding of the placement of adjectives and adverbs to rewrite the paragraph. Restore the adjectives and adverbs where you believe they belong.

4. Compare your rewritten paragraph to the one below, the original description that Luis Rodríguez gives in *Always Running*. Discuss with

a partner the ease or difficulty of this assignment and what you think made it easy or difficult. What knowledge of language did you have to use? What do you think the restored words add to the paragraph? What do you think could have been left out? Why do you suppose Rodríguez chose these words and phrases rather than others?

From *Always Running: La Vida Loca; Gang Days in L.A.*, by Luis J. Rodríguez (Willimantic, CT: Curbstone, 1993).

> Although we moved around the Watts area, the house on 105th Street near McKinley Avenue held my earliest memories, my earliest fears and questions. It was a small matchbox of a place. Next to it stood a tiny garage with holes through the walls and an unpainted barnlike quality. The weather battered it into a leaning shed. The backyard was a jungle. Vegetation appeared to grow down from the sky. There were banana trees, huge "sperm" weeds (named that because they stank like semen when you cut them), foxtails and yellowed grass. An avocado tree grew in the middle of the yard and its roots covered every bit of ground, tearing up cement walks while its branches scraped the bedroom windows. A sway of clothes on some lines filled the little bit of grassy area just behind the house. (20)

IV: Investigating Language Phenomena

Central concept: Learning through inquiry can be motivational and powerful. Teachers could follow the same sequence for all inquiry lessons on language, varying the phenomena and the texts examined.

Reading-writing connection: editing.

Benchmarks: "[using . . .] possessives [. . .] in writing" (Colorado 16)

Research base: This lesson uses two research-based strategies identified by Robert Marzano, Debra Pickering, and Jane E. Pollock as proven methods to increase student achievement—identifying similarities and differences and generating and testing hypotheses. The theoretical perspective comes from the work of Lev Vygotskii regarding concept development. He contended that, for concepts to really "stick," learners need to be conscious of their learning; concept acquisition requires "an act of mind." As students compare the features of words in various categories, assign additional words to existing categories, and eventually create categories, they develop an understanding of a concept rather than memorize a rule. In generating rules to explain the assignment of words and phrases to a particular category and testing their rules against other examples, they make conscious their subconscious knowledge of language conventions.

Inquiry Sequence (Teacher Planning)

1. Identify the focus phenomenon, such as apostrophes.
2. Initially, provide students with examples and nonexamples of conventional use, such as the following, and ask them to create the rules that would explain each set:

book's binding	books binding
Joneses' house	Joneses house
teacher's gradebook	teachers gradebook
and so on	and so on

3. To reinforce and develop the concept of using apostrophes to indicate singular and plural possessives, follow the sequence in "Directions for Students." You could substitute any language phenomena and follow the same steps—give students a data set (see Figure 10.1.), ask them to write sentences that use the example words, continue the patterns, create or identify rules (more experienced students could easily create the rules; students who need more support should be successful at matching the rules), write sentences to exchange, and find examples in their reading outside of class.

Singular	Plural
book	books
teacher	teachers
Mrs. Rodriguez	The Rodriguezes
Mr. Jones	The Joneses
Singular Possessive	**Plural Possessive**
book's	books'
teacher's	teachers'
Mrs. Rodriguez's	the Rodriguezes'*
Mr. Jones's	the Joneses'

* *The Chicago Manual of Style* deems this an awkward construction because it is a multisyllabic Spanish surname and recommends recasting the phrase to read "of the Rodriguezes."

Figure 10.1.

Directions for Students

1. Write three sentences of your own, correctly using words from at least three categories.

2. Add two more words to each box, following the established pattern.

3. Match one of the following rules with the correct box by labeling it after the rule with the name of the box.

   a. For names ending in silent *s*, *z*, or *x* the possessive can generally be formed in the usual way [by adding *'s*] without suggesting an incorrect pronunciation. _____

   b. The possessive of singular nouns is formed by the addition of an apostrophe and an *s*, and the possessive of plural nouns (except for a few irregular plurals) by the addition of an apostrophe only. _____

4. Write five sentences to exchange in class. Follow this model of identifying the word to go in the blank, but use your own words for the sentence: "I couldn't find the _____ (teacher) instructions for how to do the homework." Note that the word in parentheses is the singular form of the noun you want in the blank. In this case, the correct answer would be "teacher's."

5. For homework, due in three days, find five examples of possessives formed correctly and two incorrect examples. Be ready to post those examples on the class bulletin board.

Selecting Material

The first three activities use fiction and memoir; the fourth can be used with any written text. Teaching grammar in the context of reading works with any kind of material because what matters is the approach, not the material. However, having students read several types of material is essential. If our goal is to immerse students in language so that they can understand and write in a variety of ways for a variety of audiences, we need to provide experiences with both familiar and unfamiliar genres. As students are learning to use and name reading strategies such as setting purposes or revising meaning, they should read comprehensible text at or slightly beyond their comfort level. When meaning is readily accessible, attention to craft can take precedence.

When we want students to write in genres unfamiliar to them, they need to read those genres, discuss the language structures used in them, and try out similar structures in their writing. Examining one aspect of craft across the work of several writers, such as the use of simple sentences or metaphors, helps students understand the role that grammar can play in their comprehension and in the writer's construction of meaning. While writers do not set out to include a certain number of sentences of a particular type, a reader's analysis of the text provides clues to the relationship between language structure and meaning and a general sense of the language possibilities writers might employ.

Focusing on English Language Learners

English language learners understand that languages have a structure even though they do not possess a native speaker's innate knowledge of the structure of English. They are more likely to learn the grammar of English through a combination of immersion in language-rich environments, learning in social contexts, and instructional scaffolding that supports acquiring language proficiency. MaryCarmen Cruz advises, "What we can do is educate ourselves about the characteristics of second-language learners and follow best practices that assist English language learners and native speakers" (17). Using tools for constructing and communicating meaning such as graphic organizers and patterns for writing such as sentence beginnings and "structures for discourse" (15) supports all learners. While there is much more to know about assisting English language learners in speaking, listening, reading, and writing, Cruz's words offer a starting point for our further exploration and education.

"What am I supposed to do about grammar?"

Alice might begin rethinking how she teaches reading and writing with a small change. She already knows that teaching grammar in isolation does not work, and she has not felt successful teaching grammar in the context of students' writing. Adding attention to language structure as she teaches strategies for reading literature may provide the instruction students need. Alice's assisting students to be aware of the role of language in all of our communication will help students better construct and communicate knowledge, information, and ideas. Putting language at the center of an English language arts curriculum benefits all learners.

Appendix: Definitions and Research on Grammar and Writing

Definitions of Grammar

Most writers identify three to five meanings of *grammar* (see Hartwell; Kolln; Noguchi; Weaver). In *Teaching Grammar in Context*, Constance Weaver focuses on four major senses of *grammar:*

- Grammar as a description of syntactic structure
- Grammar as prescriptions for how to use structures and words
- Grammar as rhetorically effective use of syntactic structures
- Grammar as the functional command of sentence structure that enables us to comprehend and produce language (2)

These senses underlie a connection between grammar and writing in their emphasis on sentence structure and usage.

The authors of *Grammar Alive!* say that "the term *grammar* refers to two kinds of knowledge about language. One is *subconscious knowledge*, the language ability that children develop at an early age without being taught. [. . .] The other kind of knowledge is the *conscious understanding* of sentences and texts that can help students improve their reading and writing abilities by building on that subconscious knowledge. This conscious understanding includes

- knowing the parts of sentences and how they work together,
- knowing how sentences connect with one another to build meaning, and
- understanding how and why we use language in different ways in different social situations" (Haussamen, Benjamin, Kolln, and Wheeler xiii).

This broader definition supports the authors' efforts to weave language awareness and instruction throughout the curriculum.

In his study of the limits and possibilities of teaching grammar to improve writing, Rei Noguchi initially restricts *grammar* "to traditional grammar since this type of grammar is the one most commonly taught in the classroom." Then within that category he "restrict[s] the term to mean the set of categories, functions, and rules (both descriptive and prescriptive) that teachers commonly employ to describe a sentence and its parts. [. . .] Teachers of traditional grammar, when analyzing sentences, employ such categories as noun, verb, phrase, and clause and such functions as subject, direct object, and predicate nominative" (1–2).

Noguchi might have added that these are the categories and functions often found in the language of English language arts standards. Take, for example, a benchmark for grades 11 and 12 from Colorado: "use phrases and clauses for purposes of modification [. . .] in writing and speaking" (17). California's Written and Oral English Language Conventions for grades 9 and 10 include "[i]dentify and correctly use clauses (e.g., main and subordinate), phrases (e.g., gerund, infinitive, and participial), and mechanics of punctuation (e.g., semicolons, colons, ellipses, hyphens)" (62). "Some Questions and Answers about Grammar," prepared by NCTE's Assembly for the Teaching of English Grammar, notes that

> Four of the twelve [NCTE/IRA *Standards for the English Language Arts*] call on the students' understanding of language and sentence structure:
>
> - Standard #3 refers to the range of strategies and abilities students should use to comprehend and appreciate texts, and among these is their understanding of *sentence structure*.
>
> - Standard #4 explains that students should adjust their spoken and written language for different audiences and purposes, and these adjustments include changes in the *conventions and style of language.*
>
> - Standard #6 states that students should "apply *knowledge of language structure, language conventions* (e.g., spelling and punctuation) to create and critique both print and nonprint texts." (Italics added.)
>
> - Standard #9 calls for students to "develop an understanding of and respect for diversity in *language use, patterns, and dialects* across cultures, ethnic groups, geographic regions, and social roles." (Italics added.) Understanding basic grammar can help students see the patterns of different languages and dialects. (1–2)

This explanation of the NCTE/IRA standards is consistent with the two definitions of grammar provided by the authors of *Grammar Alive!* Indeed, members of the Assembly for the Teaching of English Grammar prepared both publications.

The suggestions for teaching grammar in contexts for writing that appear in this chapter address various state and national language arts standards but focus more on language structure than on the diversity of language uses since an understanding of language variation is less often taught as a component of writing.

Relationship of Isolated Grammar Instruction to Improvement in Writing

It may seem that, if students do not demonstrate an understanding of language structure, conventions, and usage in their writing, then explicit teaching of structure, conventions, and usage is needed. But this is not how language is learned. Writers gain control over their written texts through wide reading, practice writing, and focused instruction on just what is needed.

Some teachers—but not all—know and believe the research conclusions declaring that teaching grammar in isolation is not only ineffective in improving students' writing but may be harmful in that grammar instruction and drills take time away from actual writing (Braddock; Hillocks, *Research*). George Hillocks Jr. offered a comprehensive review of the studies since the early 1960s and concluded:

> None of the studies reviewed for the present report provides any support for teaching grammar as a means of improving composition skills. If schools insist upon teaching the identification of parts of speech, the parsing or diagramming of sentences, or other concepts of traditional grammar (as many still do), they cannot defend it as a means of improving the quality of writing. (*Research* 138)

After a thorough review of this body of research and of additional studies in the United States and New Zealand, Weaver concluded that "Overall, *it is difficult to escape the conclusion that teaching formal, isolated grammar to average or heterogeneous classes, perhaps even to highly motivated students in elective classes, makes no appreciable difference in their ability to write, to edit, or to score better on standardized tests*" (26; italics in original).

One practice that seems to make a difference in the quality of written compositions is sentence combining (Hillocks 1995). Hillocks explains that "[w]hile sentence combining is related to grammar, it is quite different. It does not deal with naming the parts of speech or sentences. Rather, it focuses on the procedures of putting phrases, clauses, and sentences together" (222). This emphasis on the procedures, on experiential learning rather than identification of terms, seems to be key. William Strong, who has been influential in introducing sentence combining to secondary school teachers and students, contends that "language learners construct three kinds of knowledge about language. There is *declarative knowledge*, a knowledge about matters like parts of speech or cleft transformations; there is *procedural knowledge*, a knowledge of how to make effective transitions or reduce clauses to phrases;

and there is *conditional knowledge,* a knowledge of when to apply the other two types" (29; italics in original).

Approaches to teaching grammar in contexts for writing must require students to employ all three kinds of knowledge about language. *Declarative knowledge* may come well after students have developed *procedural knowledge,* but they need both if they are to develop metalinguistic awareness, the ability to talk about language. "Going meta," as James Britton said to me during a tutorial in Oxford in 1983, is the stage where we have what *The Literacy Dictionary* calls "an awareness and knowledge of one's mental processes such that one can monitor, regulate, and direct them to a desired end" (Harris and Hodges 153). Proficient readers, for example, are aware of when they do not understand what they are reading, and they have "fix-up" strategies that help them adjust their comprehension. Skilled writers need to "go meta" to know when and how to use language for specific purposes and audiences. It is no wonder that instruction that focuses on identification of terms through drill and workbook exercises comes up short in improving writing.

11 Join the E-Generation: Integrating Computers into the Writing Classroom

Nancy Patterson

I remember when it hit me. It was the day before winter vacation, always a chaotic day in a middle school. My students came into the classroom decked in ribbons and carrying assorted gifts and bags of candy they'd received from friends. I had anticipated that it would be difficult to get them settled, but, to my surprise, my students plunked their overloaded book bags on the tables, grabbed their project folders, and headed for the computer lab. I thought they would beg for a "free day" or complain that there was no movie scheduled for the class period. But they walked down the hall, entered the computer lab, and logged onto the computers. For the rest of the class period I heard only the usual clatter of fingers on keyboards and exclamations when a student found just the right image or uploaded a page successfully to a Web site. Rather than hearing complaints, I heard the mellow sounds of students highly engaged in a meaningful task.

That's when I knew I had discovered something very important. Computers are a powerful tool for helping students see themselves as writers, and for helping them understand that writing is a recursive process in which they can flow from drafting to revising to editing to drafting to prewriting to drafting to revising, etc. Computers put students in charge of their own processes.

Flickers of Light

William Costanzo regards the computer screen as one of the changing sites of literacy today. Costanzo explains, "Anyone who has written with a computer knows that language on the screen seems different from language on the page. It seems more flexible, more fluid, more akin to the flickering of light than to the fixity of print" (11). Costanzo refers to the fact that electronic text can be changed very easily, and that the text is really nothing more than electronic flickers of light and dark. But these flickers can spark highly meaningful and engaging writing events for students in classrooms.

Word Processing

When I first asked students to use computers for writing, I made the mistake of having them write their first drafts by hand and only use the computer for their final copies. But I was only thinking of the computer as a glorified typewriter. I wasn't thinking of it as a tool that would help students process words, process language.

Many teachers immediately think about word processing when they think of computers and writing. And it should be no surprise that word processing and writing process pedagogy have arrived at about the same time. Because writing is a mode of expression unique to each individual, no two people compose a piece of writing in quite the same way, either; each individual's processes are also unique. To approach writing in the classroom as a series of fixed steps in a linear progression (prewriting, drafting, editing, revising, publishing) we fail to tap into the real power of writing as a process. Computers not only can help students engage more fully in their authentic processes, but they can help teachers imagine the complexity of the processes more fully as well. When we ask students to write their drafts first by hand, we are failing to recognize, first, the power of word processing, and, second, the power that rests in each student, regardless of proficiency, to become "in charge" of his or her writing. In other words, we are imposing ourselves as teachers too much into students' writing processes. So not only can word processing help support students through their writing processes, it can help teachers take on the more meaningful role of facilitator.

There are some key elements or steps that individual writers generally take, and our students will become better writers if we let them wrestle with those elements in an environment that is both demanding and nurturing. Generally, a writer goes through some sort of invention or prewriting process, what Fran Claggett calls "visioning," during which he or she decides what to write, and begins organizing materials, thoughts, and strategies in order to prepare for the next step. The next step may include more brainstorming or collecting of ideas. Or it could be a launch into drafting. During the drafting process the author writes the piece. But also during the drafting process, the author will often critically read his or her piece, return to the invention process in order to better organize his or her thoughts and information, and even venture into the next phase of the process, which is revising.

Revising involves revisioning of the piece. Again, during the revising process, an author may return to the invention process and may return to the drafting process. At some point in the process a writer will also edit. This means the author may go back and correct any surface errors, or he or she may substitute one word for another. During the editing stage, however, a writer may continue to revise, draft, or even invent. Generally, the final stage of the process involves publication, which means that the piece of writing gains a larger audience. However, that does not mean the author stops revising, drafting, inventing, or even editing. The stages of the process are fluid and recursive rather than linear and lockstep (see, for example, "The Writing Process"). The computer seems uniquely capable of assisting writers in that fluid recursive process.

When I first asked students to compose wholly at the computer, I was annoyed when some wrote stories using a forty-eight-point font. "I've got a seventeen-page story!" someone would announce. And I was dismayed when a student wrote an entire piece in a font that had little dancing flecks in each word. I could barely read the text. But what I eventually realized was that students were playing with textuality and this sense of play was actually nudging them to take risks with their writing. Yes, I asked them to print out their pieces in a font that didn't waste paper and was easier to read. But textual play is very important and we have to remember that sometimes students need to simply play around with the bells and whistles on a computer, especially if they have not had much experience composing at a computer in the past. The play should quickly merge into meaningful work that helps students take a few risks with their writing. I was always amazed when I watched students log onto a computer, pull up a piece in process, and begin to read what they had written previously. And in the process of reading, they began editing and revising. It warmed my heart, especially when I remembered the years when revising seemed so odious to students.

Peer Response

The power of word processing doesn't rest in the act of electronic composing alone, however. Terry Tannacito of Frostburg State University in Maryland found that students enjoyed sharing electronic drafts of their writing and that most of the comments submitted electronically by peer-response groups were supportive and helpful and that the re-

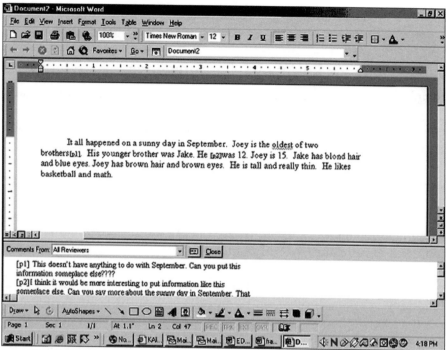

Figure 11.1. Here we see the beginning of a story. Inserted into the text are brackets with p1 and p2 markers that indicate there is a comment. When a student moves the cursor over these brackets, a comment appears. When reviewers insert comments, they place the cursor where they want to comment, go to the toolbar at the top of the screen, and select the comment feature. They then type their comments in a window that appears, usually at the bottom of the screen.

visions that came about as a result of the electronic response resulted in stronger pieces of writing. He pointed out, though, that electronic peer response groups work best when the classroom environment is supportive and nurturing (par. 15ff).

Peer-response groups can use the "comment feature" in word processing programs. Students send their piece of writing to members of the response group, who read the piece and insert comments directly into the text through the comment feature (see Figure 11.1).

Students make their comments, save the file, and then send it back to the writer as an attachment. If sending attachments is a problem, or students do not have access to e-mail at school, members of the peer-response group can visit the writers' computers, type their comments and save the text. Writers can then revisit their computers and read the comments from the members of their response group.

Tapping into the Power of E-Conversations

Plainly, then, word processing isn't the only computer application teachers can integrate into their classrooms. Many of our students have discovered the charms of electronic conversation. It is easy to dismiss such things as e-mail, instant messaging, and chat rooms as "corrupters" of written language. People often use a type of shorthand that some English teachers find annoying; at the same time that we are hoping to help our students become fluent in formal written language, our students may be substituting "r" for "are" or failing to attend to conventions of spelling, punctuation, and capitalization. But we have to remember that language is social and that different social environments have different conventions.

One way to challenge students to use online conversation is, as mentioned earlier, through sharing drafts of writing electronically and getting responses from peers. Students in peer-response groups can e-mail emerging drafts to each other and get feedback. They can either attach their pieces to an e-mail message and use the comment feature, or they can copy a poem or the lead to a story and send it to every person in a response group. Members of the group can send their replies to everyone in the group. In this way, students use written language to respond to written language. Students responding to other students' work are engaged in purposeful writing and critical reading that builds critical thinking and writing skills.

E-Mail Discussion Lists

Another way to integrate electronic conversations into the classroom is through e-mail discussion lists. Teachers can form these groups either through the school's mail server, or through one of several free discussion list sites on the Internet.

Many school districts bar students from accessing e-mail during school, but e-mail discussion lists are such wonderful vehicles for student thinking that schools might want to reconsider their stance on student e-mail. My eighth-grade classes each formed an e-mail discussion list for just their class. I used one of the free services that inserts advertising in the messages because although I found these ads distracting, and truly question the role that advertising should have in a school environment, I could not ignore the fact that my students were engaged in vibrant conversations about the material they were reading.

E-mail discussion lists can function in much the same way as response journals. Teachers can help students focus their conversation about a novel the whole class is reading, for example, by asking one or two questions that students can respond to. The wonderful thing about the e-mail discussion is that everyone's responses are read by the entire class. Each member of the class receives all e-mail messages sent to the list. Teachers can ask open-ended questions that are designed to prompt students to think and write. Questions like "Who is your favorite character and why is that character your favorite?" or "What advice would you give a character in the story and why would you give that advice?" can help students engage with a text. And because everyone's responses can be read, students can learn from one another. I have often encouraged students to find ways that they could disagree with another student, and showed them how they could politely do that. They learned very quickly and truly enjoyed the conversations that arose during those very civilized disagreements.

When I began using e-mail discussion in my classroom, I worried that some students would be reluctant to share. I found that just the opposite was true. Students who had remained silent during "regular" class discussion suddenly came alive online.

In order for e-mail discussion lists to work, students all need to have e-mail addresses and teachers need to provide time for students to both write and read e-mail messages. Some students have access to computers at home, but other students do not. My classroom had two networked and Internet-connected computers, and students could access their e-mail if they had finished a project, or during reading workshop. Students would merely have to sign up for five- to ten-minute slots, log on, read their mail, and write their responses. If students were in the computer lab for a class period, they could all check their e-mail during the last fifteen minutes of the class. Since I was also a member of the e-mail discussion list, I could monitor the conversation and respond as well. I required that students respond to the list at least once a week, and write at least a paragraph each time.

Because e-mail is a "quick writing space," I viewed the messages as I would a learning journal. Spelling and other surface issues took a back seat to meaning. I did not want students stifling their responses because they had to attend to correctness issues. There were many other times during the class when correctness was important.

Some teachers have found "distribution lists" helpful when it is too difficult to set up an e-mail discussion list. E-mail distribution lists are created when a user types in multiple e-mail addresses in a message. Students can either place part of the draft they are working on in the message itself, or send whole drafts as attachments. The message goes out to everyone listed on the address line of the message. To respond, users click on the "reply all" button or link in their e-mail program.

Telementors

Ted Nellen, who teaches high school English in New York City, uses the Internet to full advantage when it comes to responding to student writing. His students have "cyber-mentors," people who respond to individual students' writing, many of whom live far away from New York City. A cyber-mentor views a student's drafts posted to the student's Web site (which will be discussed later in this chapter). Students and mentors correspond via e-mail about the strengths of a particular piece of writing and share suggestions. Students write for the real audience of the Internet and the real audience of a significant partner in learning.

In the explanation of telementoring that appears on his Web site, Ted writes:

> Telementoring is quite simple actually. It is mentoring via the internet. We use the web and email. The telementor has decided to assist another in the process of learning and growing. The other is this case is a scholar in my cyber english class in nyc. These scholars are 9th graders in Information Technology High School in Long Island City, Queens, NY. Queens is the most culturally diverse community in the world and ITHS is a perfect reflection of that diverse community. (par. 3)

Ted goes on to point out that peer review is the first tenet of scholarship and the Internet allows for a very dynamic form of peer review in which reviewers read a student's Web site and then respond using e-mail.

No E-Mail?

Although it can be a powerful learning tool, some schools are reluctant to allow students access to e-mail. This is unfortunate. But if that is the case, rather than ask students to send reviewed papers as attachments, they can, as described earlier, simply ask another student to sit at their computer, critically read a piece in progress, and make comments using the comment feature. Students could move within a small peer-response group, reading and commenting on pieces written by members of the group.

Bulletin Boards and Web Forums

Some teachers may decide that bulletin boards or Web forums work better for online conversations. Pat Schulze, a high school teacher in Yankton, South Dakota, asks her students to participate in such a Web forum. She divided the classes into small groups, each with a name like "Brown Trout" or "Chinook Salmon" so that students could discuss the book *A River Runs Through It*. Figure 11.2 shows the bulletin board as students were getting used to the technology and beginning the reading and responding process.

Dawn Hogue, who teaches in Sheboygan Falls, Wisconsin, also uses a Web forum. And, like Pat Schulze's students, Dawn's discuss a whole-class novel, *Speak*, by Laurie Halse Anderson. Figures 11.3 and 11.4 show how Dawn uses the Web forum to guide her ninth-grade students as they discuss *Speak* online.

Not only do Dawn's students discuss a powerful novel, but they learn important lessons about the conventions and customs of online communication as well.

Blogs

E-mail discussion lists and bulletin boards have been around for many years. But new on the classroom scene are blogs—Web logs. These are

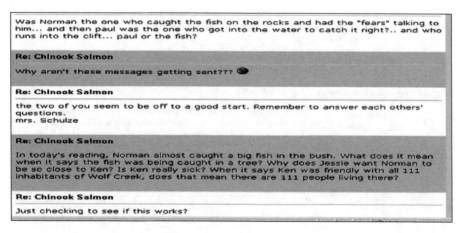

Figure 11.2. Here we can see students trying out the Web forum to see how it works, but we can also see them beginning their conversations about the novel *A River Runs Through It*. (Used with permission.)

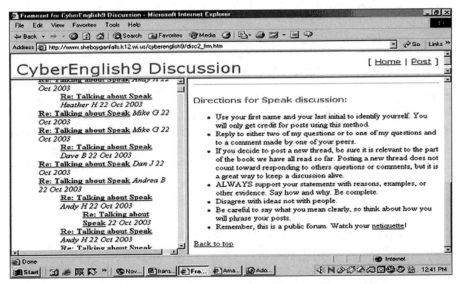

Figure 11.3. Notice that Dawn is careful about maintaining students' ano-
nymity online. She also establishes the rules for the discussion and reminds
students that they are part of a public forum. (Used with permission.)

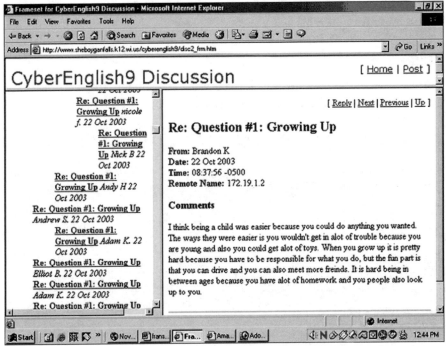

Figure 11.4. Here we see one of the responses to a question Dawn poses to
her class. Notice that this is a "quickwrite" in which meaning is more important at the moment than correctness. (Used with permission.)

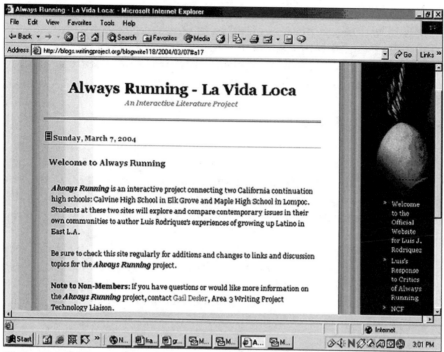

Figure 11.5. The opening screen to the *Always Running* blog site welcomes members of the blogging community created by two high school classrooms. The opening screen also provides links to Web sites related to the novel the students read. (Used with permission.)

frequently updated Web pages that feature dated entries that often look like diary or journal entries. The most recent entries are usually at the top. Gail Desler, who teaches at Calvine High School in Oak Grove, California, asks students to post to a blog hosted by the National Writing Project. Students in her class at Calvine, and students in another class, in Lompoc, California, write responses to Luis Rodríguez's popular book *Always Running: La Vida Loca; Gang Days in L.A.* (Willimantic, CT: Curbstone, 1993), which we also saw used in Chapter 10. Figure 11.5 shows the opening screen to the blog where students write their responses.

Gail's role as a technology liaison for the Area 3 Writing Project in California allows her to use blog space with the National Writing Project. But teachers can also find free blog spaces on the Internet by typing "blogs" into a search engine. Many blogging sites are set up especially for schools or classrooms. Most blogging sites allow teachers to create a "members only" rule so that only students in a particular class can log in. Some teachers might want each student to have his or her own blog, to use as a personal response journal or as a place to post pieces of writing in progress. Teachers would have access to the students' blogs and would be able to see evolving drafts of pieces of writing. Students could also then discuss the processes they use as they compose and reflect on their finished products.

Web Building Projects

Perhaps one of the most powerful ways to integrate technology into writing is to ask students to build their own Web sites. Ted Nellen, Dawn Hogue, and Pat Schulze require their students to create their own Web sites where they post essays, stories, projects, journal entries, and drafts of pieces in progress. These Web sites become, then, online portfolios or "Webfolios."

Pat Schulze's students create multigenre Web sites that move beyond the usual personal narrative essay and explore memoir using many different genres. Their work, like that of Ted Nellen's students in New York City, is accessible to everyone. By making their work public, students in these "cyber English" classes develop a strong sense of audience.

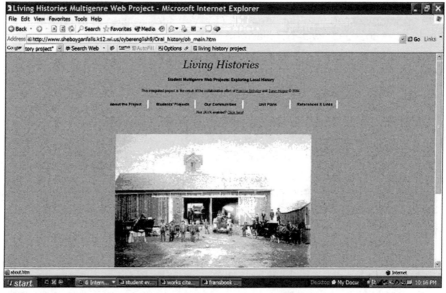

Figure 11.6. The opening screen for Pat Schulze's and Dawn Hogue's Living History Project. Students in South Dakota and Wisconsin investigate the histories of their communities and publish their writing on this Web site. (Used with permission.)

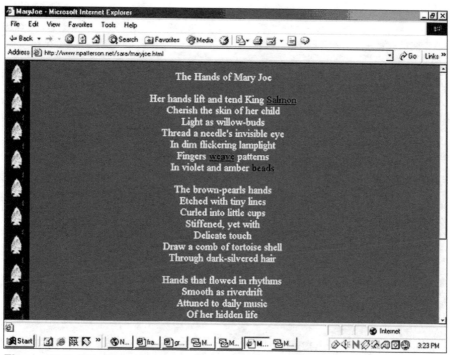

Figure 11.7. This opening screen links to information about salmon fishing, weaving, and beading. Each of those screens links to other information. (Used with permission.)

Both Dawn and Pat have challenged their students to explore local history and their Living History Project, also multigenred, immerses students in the cultures of their individual areas—Yankton, South Dakota, and Sheboygan Falls, Wisconsin (see Figure 11.6).

But students can also create Web sites that delve into a single topic. For example, students could choose a poem as their opening screen and then use key words and phrases in the poem as links to other screens that annotate or explain those key words and phrases. Figure 11.7 shows just such a screen, created by an eighth-grade student as part of an integrated project that linked language arts with history.

Figure 11.7 illustrates the application of a number of skills. The poem, "The Hands of Mary Joe," by Mary TallMountain, talks about the life of a Native American woman belonging to the Athabaskan tribe. Notice that the student used a background that fits that topic. Another screen, accessed by clicking on the word "salmon," talks about the role that salmon fishing played in some Native American cultures (Figure 11.8).

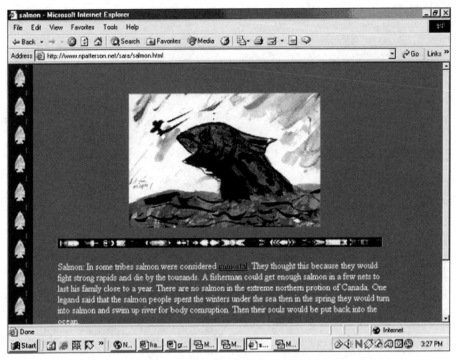

Figure 11.8. When a reader clicks on the word *salmon* in the opening screen, she or he finds a page that provides more information about the role of salmon in some Native American cultures. The page also provides links to other screens in the site. (Used with permission.)

Poetry annotation helps students grasp the concept of "linkability" and places them in an environment where they have to think not only like a writer, but also like a reader. They have to anticipate where their reader might become confused and adjust their writing in order to solve that anticipated problem. And, in the process of annotating their poems, they learn the technology skills needed to create simple Web sites.

Students studying biographies can also build Web sites based on the subjects of their biographies. In my middle school, the biography unit has been a joint project between the social studies department and the English department. History teachers provide students with a note-taking guide so that when they read something in their biography that dealt with what was going on in the country at the time their person lived, they can write those details on the "State of the Country" page in their packet. They did the same thing for family details, obstacles the person encountered, successes, etc. The packet also helped students sort

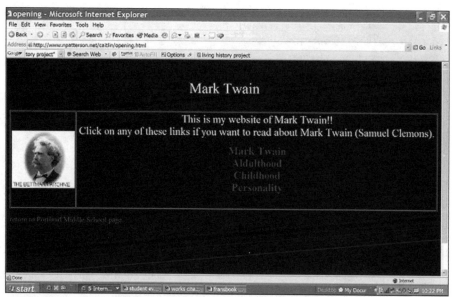

Figure 11.9. Notice the major categories that have become links into this student's biography web. The note-taking packet provided the support for students as they read their biographies and investigated Web sites. (Used with permission.)

information when they conducted further research on the Internet. When students began building their Web sites, they could organize their sites according to their note-taking packet, or they could create their own plans. Many students used the general categories established in the packet. Figure 11.9 shows the opening screen for a Web site about Mark Twain.

Not all students used the note-taking packet in this way, however, and it is important for teachers to allow students to develop their own plans for their Web sites. Figure 11.10 shows how another student organized a site about Thomas Edison.

What Does It All Mean?

Computers allow us to break out of the traditional approach to writing, the approach that privileges product over process. In an age where packaged writing programs, formulas, and standardized tests seem to place teachers more in the role of technician than teacher, computers may help bring about a new age. But computers alone will not overcome the voiceless monotony of formulaic writing or the lockstep of packaged writing programs. Computers are not fancy typewriters to be

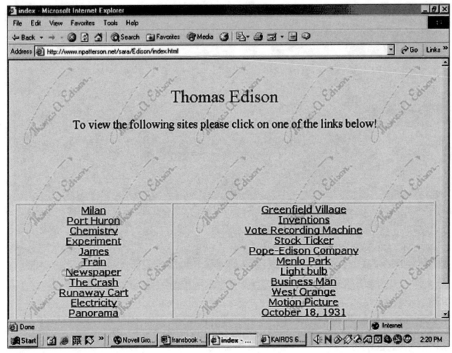

Figure 11.10. The student who created this opening screen chose not to follow the note-taking guide, but instead used specific topics within Thomas Edison's life to guide the choices she provided for readers. (Used with permission.)

used only in the final stages of a piece of writing. And computers cannot take the place of solid writing instruction. But when students are allowed to make choices about their writing, allowed to take risks and forge ahead in a direction they, rather than a teacher or some "rule book" about writing, have decided on, and allowed to write to an audience that they can in some way envision, then computers can be a marvelously supportive tool.

Computers bring to us a means of communicating beyond the walls of a school, a means of connecting to information and people in a way that is new and exciting. Not since the printing press has the world witnessed a technology that can bring about so many changes, not only in our lives, but in our classrooms. Ellin Oliver Keene and Susan Zimmerman, in their wonderful book *Mosaic of Thought: Teaching Comprehension in a Reader's Workshop,* stress that meaning happens when we connect what we read to other works that we have read, to our knowledge about ourselves, and to our knowledge about the world. Computers can help us make those connections.

Afterword: "The Truth of the Thing"

The truth of the thing
        lies inside us,
                but no power on earth can force it.
    The Art of Writing: Lu Chi's Wen Fu

T he truth of the thing": That line from Lu Chi's *Wen Fu* takes us to what the ancient Chinese called the *mindheart*, making no distinction between the intellect and emotion. To be a teacher of writing, to be a teacher of anything, requires the fusion of what we have learned and what we know. As writing teachers we learn from our mentors and our students, from our own experience as struggling writers, from our deep satisfaction when we see in a student's eyes, as she hands us a poem or a research project or a piece of her life in a memoir, the knowledge that it is a piece well written. As writing teachers we take what we can from books, from conferences, from colleagues, shaping that external information into our own felt knowledge of how best to help our students become, as we stated at the beginning of this book, confident and effective writers. Writers are, as we have tried to demonstrate, constant decision makers. As teachers, we are also constantly making critical decisions: Leif Fearn put it well when he wrote, "We must decide what to teach, to whom, how, for how long, and to what end. What we're doing until we make those decisions is merely conducting activities."

The focus must be on what "we" as the professionals decide, not on what external forces decide. Decisions for classroom teachers today are difficult because of the administrative and political forces that mandate both content and approach. But good teachers have always found ways to be true to their own knowledge of what is best for their students, and we have some powerful teacher testimonies to that effect. To do what you know is the most powerful way to help students learn means being truly professional, being true to the "truth of the thing."

What we have tried to do in this book is convey some of the knowledge that has contributed to our own mindheart understanding of what it means to be a writing teacher. Our hope is that those of you who are teachers will find some things here that resonate with you and that, perhaps, expand your own understanding of a subject that we continue to explore, to refine, to revision.

Works Cited

Atwell, Nancie. *In the Middle: New Understandings about Writing, Reading, and Learning.* 2nd ed. Portsmouth, NH: Boynton, 1998.

Axelrod, Rise B., and Charles R. Cooper. *The St. Martin's Guide to Writing.* 3rd ed. New York: St. Martin's, 1991.

Braddock, Richard, Richard Lloyd-Jones, and Lowell Schoer. *Research in Written Composition.* Champaign, IL: NCTE, 1963.

Britton, James N. *Language and Learning: The Importance of Speech in Children's Development.* 2nd rev. ed. Harmondsworth, Eng.: Penguin, 1992.

California Dept. of Education. California Assessment Program Handbooks, Grades 8 and 12. Sacramento: California State Dept. of Education Publications, 1990.

———. "Written and Oral English Language Conventions." *English–Language Arts Content Standards for California Public Schools, Kindergarten through Grade Twelve.* Ed. Faye Ong. Sacramento: California Dept. of Education, 1998. 24 May 2004 www.cde.ca.gov/re/pn/fd/documents/english-language-arts.pdf.

Chandler, Daniel. "Introduction to Genre Theory." Univ. of Wales, Aberystwyth. 1997. 7 Feb. 2005 http://www.aber.ac.uk/media/Documents/intgenre/intgenre.html.

Claggett, Fran. *A Measure of Success: From Assignment to Assessment in English Language Arts.* Portsmouth, NH: Heinemann, 1996.

———. "Poetry as a Window into Culture." Asilomar English Conference 50. Pacific Grove, Calif. 23 Sept. 2000.

Claggett, Fran, with Joan Brown. *Drawing Your Own Conclusions: Graphic Strategies for Reading, Writing, and Thinking.* Portsmouth, NH: Boynton,1992.

Claggett, Fran, Louann Reid, and Ruth Vinz. *Daybook of Critical Reading and Writing, Grade 9.* Wilmington, MA: Great Source, 1999.

———. *Daybook of Critical Reading and Writing, Grade 10.* Wilmington, MA: Great Source, 1999.

———. *Learning the Landscape: Inquiry-Based Activities for Comprehending and Composing,* Portsmouth, NH: Boynton, 1996.

———. *Recasting the Text: Inquiry-Based Activities for Comprehending and Composing.* Portsmouth, NH: Boynton, 1996.

Colorado Dept. of Education. "Colorado Model Content: Standards for Reading and Writing." 2000. 24 May 2004 www.cde.state.co.us/cdeassess/standards/pdf/stan_readwrite_expect.pdf.

Cooper, Charles R. "What We Know about Genres, and How It Can Help Us Assign and Evaluate Writing." *Evaluating Writing: The Role of Teachers' Knowledge about Text, Learning, and Culture.* Ed. Charles R. Cooper and Lee Odell. Urbana, IL: NCTE, 1999.

Corbett, Edward P. J. *Classical Rhetoric for the Modern Student.* New York: Oxford UP, 1965.

———. "The Theory and Practice of Imitation in Classical Rhetoric." *College Composition and Communication* 22 (1971): 242–50.

Costanzo, William. "Reading, Writing, and Thinking in an Age of Electronic Literacy." *Literacy and Computers: The Complications of Teaching and Learning with Technology.* Ed. Cynthia L. Selfe and Susan Hilligoss. New York: MLA, 1994. 11–21.

Cruz, MaryCarmen. "Can English Language Learners Acquire Academic English?" *English Journal* 93.4 (Mar. 2004): 14–17.

D'Angelo, Frank J. "Imitation and Style." *College Composition and Communication* 24 (1973): 283–90. Rpt. as "Imitation and the Teaching of Style" in *Forum: Essays on Theory and Practice in the Teaching of Writing.* Ed. Patricia L. Stock. Upton Sinclair, NJ: Boynton, 1983.

Deutsch, Babette. *Poetry Handbook: A Dictionary of Terms.* New York: Funk, 1957.

Donaldson, Margaret. *Children's Minds.* New York: Harper, 1978.

Eschholz, Paul A. "The Prose Models Approach: Using Products in the Process." *Eight Approaches to Teaching Composition.* Ed. Timothy R. Donovan and Ben W. McClelland. Urbana, IL: NCTE, 1980. 21–36.

Fearn, Leif. Posting to CATENet discussion list. 5 Jan. 2005.

Gardner, Howard. *Frames of Mind: The Theory of Multiple Intelligences.* New York: Basic, 1983.

Gilmour, Peter. *The Wisdom of Memoir: Reading and Writing Life's Sacred Texts.* Winona, MN: Saint Mary's, 1997.

Harris, Theodore L., and Richard E. Hodges. *The Literacy Dictionary: The Vocabulary of Reading and Writing.* Newark, DE: International Reading Association, 1995.

Hartwell, Patrick. "Grammar, Grammars, and the Teaching of Grammar." *College English* 47.2 (1985): 105–27. Rpt. in *Rhetoric and Composition: A Sourcebook for Teachers and Writers.* 3rd ed. Ed. Richard L. Graves. Portsmouth: Boynton, 1990. 163–85.

Haussamen, Brock, Amy Benjamin, Martha Kolln, and Rebecca S. Wheeler. *Grammar Alive! A Guide for Teachers.* Urbana, IL: NCTE, 2003.

Hillesum, Etty. *An Interrupted Life: The Diaries, 1941–1943; and, Letters from Westerbork.* Trans. Arno Pomerans. New York: Holt, 1996.

Hillocks, George, Jr. *Research on Written Composition: New Directions for Teaching.* Urbana, IL: NCTE and NCRE, 1986.

————. *Teaching Writing as Reflective Practice*. New York: Teachers College P, 1995.

Janeczko, Paul B. *Going Over to Your Place: Poems for Each Other*. New York: Bradbury, 1987.

Keene, Ellin Oliver, and Susan Zimmerman. *Mosaic of Thought: Teaching Comprehension in a Reader's Workshop*. Portsmouth, NH: Heinemann, 1997.

Kirby, Dan, Dawn Latta Kirby, and Tom Liner. *Inside Out: Strategies for Teaching Writing*. Portsmouth, NH: Heinemann, 2004.

Kolln, Martha. "Closing the Books on Alchemy." *College Composition and Communication* 32 (1981): 139–51.

Lowenbach, Janet. "Response and Bio." *Double Room* 1 (Fall 2002/Winter 2003). 2 Mar. 2005 http://webdelsol.com/Double_Room/issue_one/JL_ResBio.html.

Marzano, Robert J., Debra Pickering, and Jane E. Pollock. *Classroom Instruction That Works: Research-Based Strategies for Increasing Student Achievement*. Alexandria, VA: Association for Supervision and Curriculum Development, 2001.

McCampbell, James F. "Using Models for Improving Composition." *English Journal* 55 (1966): 772–76.

Miles, Josephine. "What We Compose." Unpublished paper distributed to Bay Area Writing Project consultants, 1977.

NCTE's Assembly for the Teaching of English Grammar. "Some Questions and Answers about Grammar." 2004. 2 Feb. 2005 www.ncte.org/about/over/positions/category/gram/107646.htm.

Nellen, Ted. "Telementoring." Information Technology High School, Queens, NY. 2003. 10 Feb. 2005 http://www.tnellen.com/iths/tele.html.

Noguchi, Rei R. *Grammar and the Teaching of Writing: Limits and Possibilities*. Urbana, IL: NCTE, 1991.

Perrine, Laurence, and Thomas R. Arp. *Sound and Sense: An Introduction to Poetry*. 8th ed. Fort Worth: Harcourt, 1992.

Prater, Peggy. "Prose Poetry." 2001. 2 Feb. 2005 http://pw2.netcom.com/~pprater/prosepoetry.html.

Purves, Alan C., and William C. Purves. "Viewpoints: Cultures, Text Models, and the Activity of Writing." *Research in the Teaching of English* 20 (1986): 174–97.

Reiss, Donna. "Allusion, Artistry, and the Fall of Icarus." WordsWorth2 Communication and Consulting. 1999. 9 Feb. 2005 www.wordsworth2.net/resource/icarus/index.htm.

Rico, Gabriele Lusser. *Writing the Natural Way: Using Right-Brain Techniques to Release Your Expressive Powers*. Los Angeles: Tarcher, 1983.

Rico, Gabriele L., and Mary Frances Claggett. *Balancing the Hemispheres: Brain Research and the Teaching of Writing.* Berkeley: U of California, 1980.

Romano, Tom. *Blending Genre, Altering Style: Writing Multigenre Papers.* Portsmouth, NH: Boynton, 2000.

Rosenblatt, Louise M. *The Reader, the Text, the Poem: The Transactional Theory of the Literary Work.* Carbondale: Southern Illinois UP, 1978.

Spandel, Vicki. *Creating Writers through 6-Trait Writing Assessment and Instruction.* 3rd ed. Boston: Pearson, 2000.

Stein, Gertrude. "Poetry and Grammar." *Lectures in America.* 1935. Boston: Beacon, 1985. 207–46.

Stillman, Peter R. *Families Writing.* Cincinnati: Writer's Digest, 1989.

Stolarek, Elizabeth A. "Prose Modeling and Metacognition: The Effect of Modeling on Developing a Metacognitive Stance toward Writing." *Research in the Teaching of English* 28.2 (May 1994): 154–74.

Strong, William. *Coaching Writing: The Power of Guided Practice.* Portsmouth, NH: Heinemann, 2001.

Tannacito, Terry. "Teaching Professional Writing Online with Electronic Peer Response." *Kairos* 6.2 (Fall 2001). 10 Feb. 2005 http://english.ttu.edu/kairos/6.2/coverweb/de/tannacito/.

Tierney, Robert J., and P. David Pearson. "Toward a Composing Model of Reading." *Language Arts* 60.5 (May 1983): 568–80.

Vygotskii, L. S. *Thought and Language.* Ed. and trans. Eugenia Hanfmann and Gertrude Vakar. Cambridge: MIT P, 1962.

Weaver, Constance. *Teaching Grammar in Context.* Portsmouth, NH: Boynton, 1996.

"The Writing Process." Cleveland State Univ. Writing Center. N.d. 10 Feb. 2005 www.csuohio.edu/writingcenter/writproc.html.

Index

Page numbers in italics refer to illustrations; "n" after a page number indicates an endnote.

Author

Photo by Madge Holland.

Fran Claggett, after many years of teaching, is now devoting nearly full time to writing and consulting, while continuing to teach in the Osher Lifelong Learning Institute at Sonoma State University. Fran has worked with the National Council on Education and the Economy, given workshops for teachers from Alaska to Idaho to Florida, evaluated schools in Guam, and taught summer workshops in Panama and the Virgin Islands through the Bay Area Writing Project. Fran's interest in brain research led her to develop approaches to reading, writing, and thinking using metaphorical graphics. She has received many awards for her teaching and writing, including the Lifetime Achievement Award from the California Association of Teachers of English.

She has either written or co-written a number of books for teachers, including *Drawing Your Own Conclusions: Graphic Strategies for Reading, Writing, and Thinking*, with Joan Brown; *A Measure of Success: From Assignment to Assessment in English Language Arts* (winner of the 1998 James N. Britton Award); and *Learning the Landscape: Inquiry-Based Projects for Comprehending and Composing*, with Louann Reid and Ruth Vinz, as well as the *Daybooks of Critical Reading and Writing*, an innovative set of texts for high school students integrating critical reading, writing, and thinking. In addition to a volume of poetry, *Black Birds and Other Birds*, she has published poems in a number of magazines and journals, including *The Dickens* and *Artlife*.

Contributing Authors

Joan Brown currently teaches writing and literature at Solano Community College and has been actively involved in education for more than thirty years. As a teacher at Alameda High School she developed and implemented curricula for a variety of programs, served as a mentor teacher, and worked with her district to revise both its language arts curriculum and its competency testing program. At the state level she worked for the California State Department of Education to develop an integrated reading-writing assessment program, and with the California Career Educational Program to develop a student certification for vocational education programs. Nationally, Joan has worked with the America's Choice program of the National Center for Education and the Economy to develop and implement standards-based curriculum and instructional strategies that both build skills and allow students to apply what they have learned. She received the Alpha Delta Kappa Outstanding Teacher of Alameda County award and has twice been nominated by students for inclusion in *Who's Who among American Teachers*. She is a frequent presenter and consultant in schools around the country and the author of *Words of Wisdom: An Etymologically-Based Vocabulary Program* (1985), the coauthor of *Drawing Your Own Conclusions: Graphic Strategies for Reading, Writing, and Thinking* (1992), and a contributor to Fran Claggett's *A Measure of Success* (1996).

Nancy Patterson is assistant professor of education at Grand Valley State University in Grand Rapids, Michigan, and coordinates the Reading and Language Arts Program there. She chaired NCTE's Assembly on Computers in English for two years and writes "Tech Connect" for NCTE's middle school journal, *Voices from the Middle*. A former high school and middle school English teacher, she has a PhD in English from Michigan State University, where she served as the technology liaison for the Red Cedar Writing Project, a National Writing Project site there. Nancy is an avid gardener who loves nothing more than to curl up with a good book, listen to the breeze stir the tall miscanthus grass, and drink in the heady scent of the lavender that blooms all summer in her garden. She also sings and finds wonderful parallels between singing and writing. Both, she finds, demand close attention to process rather than product.

Louann Reid, professor of English at Colorado State University and current editor of *English Journal*, taught junior and senior high English, drama, and speech for nineteen years. At CSU, she specializes in secondary school English education, teaching undergraduate and graduate courses in composition, adolescents' literature, reading, and theories of teaching literature. With Fran Claggett and Ruth Vinz, she is the author of two inquiry-based textbooks, *Learning the Landscape* and *Recasting the Text,* and the *Daybooks of Critical Reading and Writing* for grades 9 through 12. She has coedited two books for secondary school teachers, *Rationales for Teaching Young Adult Literature* and *Reflective Activities: Connecting Teens with Texts* and has given more than 125 presentations and workshops in the United States, Germany, the Netherlands, and Australia.

*This book was typeset in Palatino and Helvetica by Electronic Imaging.
Typefaces used on the cover were Bernhard Tango and Akzidenz Grotesk.
The book was printed on 60-lb. Accent Opaque paper by Versa Press, Inc.*